I0817470

WALTER BENJAMIN

Walter Benjamin

The Pearl Diver

PETER E. GORDON

Yale
UNIVERSITY
PRESS
New Haven and London

Yale University Press books may be purchased in quantity for educational, business, or promotional use. For information, please e-mail sales.press@yale.edu (U.S. office) or sales@yaleup.co.uk (U.K. office).

Set in Janson Oldstyle type by Integrated Publishing Solutions.
Printed in the United States of America.

ISBN 978-0-300-21686-8 (hardcover)
Library of Congress Control Number: 2025942511
A catalogue record for this book is available from the British Library.

Authorized Representative in the EU: Easy Access System Europe, Mustamäe tee 50, 10621 Tallinn, Estonia, gpsr.requests@easproject.com

10 9 8 7 6 5 4 3 2 1

Frontispiece: Walter Benjamin in the Bibliothèque Nationale (Paris), 1937 (Photograph by Gisèle Freund; © IMEC, Fonds MCC, Dist. RMN-Grand Palais/Art Resource, New York)

ALSO BY PETER E. GORDON

Books

A Precarious Happiness: Adorno and the Sources of Normativity

Migrants in the Profane: Critical Theory and the Question of Secularization

Authoritarianism: Three Essays on Critical Theory
with Wendy Brown and Max Pensky

Adorno and Existence

Continental Divide: Heidegger, Cassirer, Davos

Rosenzweig and Heidegger: Between Judaism and German Philosophy

Edited Volumes

Max Weber at 100: Legacies and Prospects
with Joshua Derman

A Companion to Adorno
with Espen Hammer and Max Pensky

The Routledge Companion to the Frankfurt School
with Espen Hammer and Axel Honneth

The Cambridge History of Modern European Thought
with Warren Breckman

The Trace of God: Derrida and Religion
with Edward Baring

Weimar Thought: A Contested Legacy
with John McCormick

The Modernist Imagination: Essays in Intellectual History and Critical Theory
with Warren Breckman et al.

The Cambridge Companion to Modern Jewish Philosophy
with Michael Morgan

CONTENTS

PROLOGUE

The Final Days

Gnädige Frau. "DEAR LADY." Before her stood a man with graying hair and thick glasses. "Please forgive the intrusion—I hope this is not an inopportune time." The morning light was still gray, and he had knocked at the door at least twice. Port-Vendres is a fishing village that sits above the Mediterranean, about five hours southwest from Marseilles by train. He had made his way there from Paris, by way of Lourdes, where he and his sister Dora had stayed for several weeks while waiting for papers of transit. It was the twenty-fifth of September 1940.

Lisa Fittko, the dark-haired woman who opened the door, was fatigued; she had been resting for a few hours before she was awakened by the knock at the door. Lisa and her husband, Hans, refugees from Berlin, had fled to France when the Nazis came to power, only to find themselves imprisoned as enemy aliens. When the German army invaded and the French government surrendered, the couple had escaped southward, where they took up the task of shepherding refugees across the border into Spain.[1]

The work was dangerous. *Gardes mobiles* now patrolled the usual routes and had orders from the Gestapo to arrest all those who lacked the proper documentation. The man at the door was well dressed. In his late forties, he had gray hair, a thick mustache, and dark blue eyes that peered out at her from behind thick eyeglasses.[2] He conducted himself with the decorum of a German professor. "Old Benjamin," she called him. "The world is falling to pieces," I thought, "but Benjamin's courtesy is unshakable."[3]

By this point in life, Walter Benjamin had established a place for himself among the most accomplished literary and cultural critics of his time. Yet a career of true security and recognition still proved elusive. Now a refugee, he had been stripped of whatever prestige he had once enjoyed, and he now was only one individual among the many hundreds of thousands who were seeking a way out of Europe as fascism tightened its grip. The rocky paths across the Pyrenees could be arduous, but on the other side lay the promise of freedom, and, if one were fortunate, the possibility of safe passage by ship across the Atlantic, perhaps to Cuba or the United States. The Fittkos would guide many refugees, and they were courageous in their work. But the lower paths were now being watched. The best alternative was *la route Lister*, an inland path that led higher and farther west across the mountains and then sloped downward to Portbou, a town nestled into the Mediterranean coastline just over the border in Catalonia. Lisa Fittko explained the details to Benjamin. "No matter," he replied, "as long as the route is safe." Then he added a caveat. "I have heart trouble, and I must walk slowly."

Port-Vendres lies about seven kilometers from Banyuls-sur-mer, a French border town that is situated below the Monts Albères, the foothills of the Pyrenees; it is famous for its vineyards and for its sweet dessert wine. The mayor of Banyuls-sur-mer was known by Fittko to be especially sympathetic to refugees, and he drew her a map of the mountain path that winds from Banyuls to Portbou. Her plan was to guide her group across the inland route. They would spend the night at an inn in Banyuls, then start out well before dawn, at four in the morning, when laborers in the vineyards would already be on their way to work. Dispersed among the workers, a small group of refugees might pass unnoticed. Benjamin was in the company of Henny Gurland and her son Joseph (known as José), fellow refugees he had met in Marseilles. (Henny Gurland succeeded in escaping to the States, where she later married the psychoanalyst Erich Fromm.) The afternoon before their departure, the four of them ventured out of town to gain some familiarity with the surroundings—they would need to navigate the first portion of the actual trip in the dark. Fittko was surprised that Benjamin was carrying a heavy-looking black briefcase. "It contains my new manuscript," he said. "But why," she asked, "have you brought it along on this scouting trip?" "Do you know, this briefcase is most important to me," he explained. "The manuscript *must* be saved. It is more important than I am."[4]

Three hours later, they arrived at their destination: a clearing where they could rest for a while before making their descent back into town. "Benjamin stretched out and closed his eyes." When they prepared to leave, he remained where he was. "I'm all right," he explained. "You three go ahead." He suggested that he would stay the night and would be waiting for them in the early morning when they returned. Fittko expressed her alarm. She had heard that there were wild animals in the vicinity, even bulls. Benjamin had no food and little protection against either the elements or unscrupulous passersby. But he was stubborn. Having already made it one third of the way across the mountains, he insisted that it made little sense to turn back.

Fittko was no less stubborn and she sat back down. "Then I'm going to stay here too." Benjamin gave her a teasing smile: "Are you going to protect me from your wild bulls, *gnädige Frau*?" Eventually Fittko gave up the effort of trying to persuade him, and she descended with the Gurlands back to Banyuls-sur-mer, leaving "old Benjamin" alone with his briefcase. He remained there through the night.

In the early morning before sunrise, Lisa Fittko and the Gurlands made the ascent once again, anxious that they might not find their companion alive. But there he was. "He sat up and looked at us amiably."[5] But something was wrong with his appearance; his eyes were ringed by dark red spots. For a moment, Fittko was seized with fear that this might be the sign of a heart attack. Benjamin hastened to explain that this was simply the result of dew on his eyeglasses; color from the frames had come off onto his face. He wiped his face with his handkerchief, and the company resumed its ascent. The *route Lister* was an old smuggler's path that ran alongside the main road but it was mostly obscured by steep outcroppings of rock. Now and then, however, the route and the road nearly converged, and at those points the company tried to remain as quiet as possible. Border police might be patrolling the road.

Benjamin walked at a deliberate pace, and about every ten minutes or so he would pause to rest. His briefcase was clearly too heavy for him to manage, so his three companions took turns sharing the burden. At one point they passed a mountainside vineyard: in the September heat the Banyuls grapes had grown dark. Fittko would later recall that this was "the first and only time that Benjamin wilted." His breath came heavy, and he announced that he could no longer go on. At this point there was no other choice: Lisa and Joseph simply dragged old Benjamin up the hill, while he looked anxiously at his briefcase. The journey continued; another four hours, perhaps more. Benjamin would pause more frequently for rests. They stopped to share their rations: Lisa had bread and tomatoes. "By your leave, *gnädige Frau*, may I serve myself?" In her memoir Fittko notes: "That was the way he was indeed, Old Benjamin and his Spanish court etiquette."[6]

After many hours they approached the peak. Lisa went ahead to scout the path and she came upon a breathtaking view. "I thought I was seeing a mirage. Far below, where we had come from, the deep-blue Mediterranean . . . on the other side, in front of us, steep cliffs fell away to a glass sheet of transparent turquoise—a second ocean? Yes, of course, it was the Spanish coast. Behind us, to the north, the semicircle of Catalonia's Roussillon . . . an autumn landscape with innumerable hues of red and yellow-gold." In her memoir she adds: "I had never seen such beauty before." Then she returned to her companions and decided that she would accompany them as far as Portbou. Benjamin was clearly at his limit. He desperately needed to quench his thirst, but the only water in sight was a greenish pool. He stooped down to drink. Fittko urged him to stop, warning that he might even catch typhoid. "Yes," he replied. "But you must understand: the worst thing that could happen is that I might die of typhoid fever—*after* I have crossed the border. The gestapo can no longer arrest me, and the manuscript will have reached safety." He drank the water, and then the group began its descent toward the town.

In Portbou they came upon a border office where the company was required to register. They would be asked to hand over their papers, including their visas of transit for both Spain and Portugal. Once they had registered, they would be free to board a train to Lisbon, where they could secure passage on an ocean liner to cross the Atlantic. Lisa Fittko would leave them there. She said farewell and then made her way back across the mountain ridge to France; in only two hours she was once again in Banyuls. Over the coming months she guided several more groups across the *route Lister*. Among those she assisted was the economist Albert Hirschman, who, in concert with the journalist Varian Fry, would help many other refugees, including the painter Marc Chagall and the political theorist Hannah Arendt. In her memoir Fittko recalls a feeling of satisfaction. "Old Benjamin and his manuscript are safe now, safe on the other side of the mountains."[7]

One would like to imagine a counter-life in which Benjamin survived. But Lisa Fittko was mistaken. Benjamin and his companions made it to the Spanish border only to be informed by the officers that a new order had just been sent from Madrid: it was forbidden to enter Spain without a *visa de sortie*, an exit visa from the French government. The irony is that this order was soon rescinded. Had the group known of the order just a few days earlier, they could have waited in Banyuls until conditions proved more opportune. Had they arrived a few days later, the order would already have been annulled, and they would have been permitted to pass. Instead, the guards informed the group that their presence on Spanish soil was illegal, and they would be remanded to the custody of the French state.

The details of what happened next can be found in a memoir by Carina Birman, who, before she fled south to escape the Nazi invaders, had enjoyed a distinguished career as *Conseil Juridique* at the Austrian embassy in Paris. Birman had arrived by the *route Lister* with her own little group of refugee companions, and on the final turns of the path they met "Prof. Benjamin" and his group. Together they presented themselves at a Spanish customs office, where the police captain declared that all of them were now under arrest. Birman, Benjamin, and the assembled party were brought to a hotel that was run by the police. At the hotel he was given his own room; the Gurlands were placed in a separate room, and Birman's group was given two more. Throughout this ordeal Benjamin remained silent.

Later that evening Birman was alerted to noise from another room. She found Professor Benjamin on his bed, thoroughly exhausted and "in a desolate state of mind." Birman writes as follows:

> He told me that by no means was he willing to return to the border, or to move out of this hotel. When I remarked that there was no alternative . . . , he declared that there was one for him. He hinted that he had some very effective poisonous pills with him. He was lying half naked in his bed and had his very beautiful big golden grandfather watch with open cover on the little board near him [and he was] observing the time constantly.[8]

Benjamin had come prepared: he carried with him a lethal dose of morphine in case he was arrested. He knew that the police at the border had ties to the Nazi Secret Service; to be sent back into France would mean arrest and most likely worse. Around seven in the morning, Henny Gurland was told by a member of Birman's group that Benjamin had asked to see her. She found him in his room, and he told her that he had taken the morphine the previous evening. He asked that she explain to the others that he was simply ill, and he gave her a letter that was addressed to his friends Gershom Scholem and Theodor Adorno. Then, according to Gurland, he lost consciousness. Gurland sent for a doctor and asked that the ailing man be taken to a hospital. But the doctor "refused to accept any responsibility, since Benjamin was already moribund." Benjamin died, most likely at some time in the morning on September 26, 1940.

Gurland paid for a gravesite that lasted five years. Officials were apparently under the impression that the deceased had been a Catholic and not a Jew, so Benjamin was buried in the Catholic section of the cemetery under the name of "Dr. Benjamin Walter."[9] But when Hannah Arendt herself passed through Portbou a few months later, she searched for her friend's grave and could not find it. She described the site in a letter to Scholem. "The cemetery faces a small bay directly overlooking the

Mediterranean; it is carved in stone in terraces; the coffins are also pushed into such stone walls. It is by far one of the most fantastic and most beautiful spots I have seen in my life."[10]

His gravesite may have been forgotten, but in the afterlife of memory, Benjamin has only grown in fame. Today he is celebrated among the greatest literary and cultural critics of the twentieth century. Still, one may feel tempted to look upon his tragic death as if it symbolized an end to the long and troubled history of German Jewry. This, I suggest, is a temptation we had best avoid. A certain fashion in existential philosophy would tell us that death stands as the singular truth of the human being. But this is little more than a hollow cliché. No life is defined by its death. Nor can the achievements of an entire people be summarized by the story of its suffering or defeat. The life of Benjamin should be told in such a way that what we know of his end does not subtract from our esteem for what he accomplished. So let us now leave the ending aside and begin anew.

1

A Berlin Childhood

Dreamscapes

He loved to hide. Much later in life when he was no longer welcome in Germany, he began to write *A Berlin Childhood Around 1900*, a fragmentary work in which he recorded his earliest memories. At least a handful of these memories are worth repeating here. In his family home he sought out the enchanted places where he might disappear. "The child who stands behind the doorway curtain becomes something white that flutters, a ghost. The dining table under which he has crawled turns him into a wooden idol of the temple; its carved legs are four pillars. And behind the door, he is himself the door, is decked out in it like a weighty mask and, as sorcerer, will cast a spell on all who enter unawares. Not for a fairy kingdom would he be found."[1] He went on to spend much of his life in such feats of imagination; he later devoted an essay to *mimesis*, the human capacity to discern similarity between oneself and one's surroundings.

Literature became his refuge and natural habitat. Already as a child he imagined that he could hide himself within the folds of the curtains as if they were the pages of a book.

Walter Benedix Schönflies Benjamin was born on July 15, 1892, the eldest child of three. His brother Georg was born just three years later; his sister Dora six years after that. His parents were not natives to Berlin. His father Emil belonged to a line of Jewish merchants from the Rhineland, the German-speaking region far to the west where many luminaries of German literature and thought had been born, including Heinrich Heine and Karl Marx. His mother, Pauline Schönflies, came from a wealthy family that had first earned its fortunes in livestock and grain.[2] On both sides of the family Walter could claim membership in the Jewish milieu of Berlin's *haute bourgeoisie*. Although this group was in many respects still a distinctive tribe, by the end of the nineteenth century it was gradually losing its signs of distinction.

Acculturation did not always mean assimilation, and certainly not dissolution.[3] During the early years of the Enlightenment, German Jews such as Moses Mendelssohn (1729–1796) had carved out a unique place for themselves within a German society that did not always welcome their presence. In the nineteenth century poets and intellectuals such as Heinrich Heine (1797–1856) ascended to the heights of German Romantic culture; his poems were set to music by both Franz Schubert and Robert Schumann, while his essays on German philosophy and religion displayed an inimitable mix of irony and erudition. Among Jews, however, it was seldom forgotten that Heine had accepted conversion to Christianity as a necessary step for inclusion: although he dismissed it as a mere "matter of utility," he famously called his baptism an *entrebillet*, or entry ticket, to European culture.[4] Unlike Heine, however, neither Emil Benjamin nor his wife Pauline ever seriously considered such a step.

By family tradition Pauline belonged to a Reform congregation in Berlin; in marrying each other the couple paid homage to a heritage that was losing much of its stigma but also, perhaps, its necessity. No longer barred from careers that had once been legally forbidden, the Benjamins belonged to a privileged group that seldom felt either the sting of prejudice or the imperative of communal belonging. Especially for their children, the way seemed open for fashioning a future as they wished.

For the German *Bildungsbürgertum*, or educated middle class, the ideal of *Bildung* or cultural erudition still beckoned almost as brightly as it once had for Heine. And this was surely the case for the Benjamins and their extended family. Arthur Schönflies, a maternal great-uncle, had been a professor of mathematics at the University of Frankfurt; he also served as its rector. Gustav Hirschfeld, another maternal great-uncle, had once been professor of classical archaeology at the University of Königsberg. Gertrud Kolmar, a cousin on the Schönflies side, was an accomplished poet who lived in the Charlottenburg district of Berlin, not far from the house where Walter spent much of his youth.[5] (Born in 1894, just two years after Walter, she published several volumes of poetry; she was murdered in Auschwitz in 1943.) For Walter himself, even while he rejected the conventions of bourgeois society, the wish that he might achieve something of lasting importance in German culture was to become all-consuming. To his friend Gershom Scholem he later confessed that it was his goal "to be regarded as the foremost critic of German literature."[6] The crushing blow to his hopes of becoming a professor like others in his extended family could hardly deter him from pursuing this dream. As it happens, there is some evidence that the Benjamins were distantly related to Heine, whose mother was a descendent of the van Gelderns, a prominent family of court Jews from Dusseldorf; van Geldern was the same name as the Benjamins' paternal grandmother.[7] Benjamin told his friend Scholem of this link, though neither

Young Walter in Heringsdorf, at a seaside resort on the Baltic Sea, 1896

of them felt any real affinity with Heine, whose Romanticism too often lapsed into mere sentimentality.[8]

In his childhood years, the young Walter seems to have passed his time wandering in an urban dreamscape. Berlin was "a maze not only of paths but also of tunnels" in which a child could easily lose his way, as if the city were an uncharted forest. One of the most memorable events of his childhood happened when he was about eight years old. A local flood was unleashed on a deserted street and brought "torrents of water," an experience that left him with the feeling that he was "exposed to the powers of nature." If he had been lost in a "primeval forest," he wrote, he "would not have been more abandoned than here on Kurfürstenstrasse, between the columns of water." Years later, he could not recall how he had made it back from the flood to the bronze lions that flanked the doorway to his family home and whose rings appeared to him as if they were "lifebelts."[9]

Not far from his first family residence at 4 Magdeburger Platz there lay the green expanse of the Tiergarten and the zoological garden, where he could observe exotic creatures such as ostriches, and the hippopotamus that "dwelt in its pagoda like a tribal sorcerer on the point of merging bodily with the demon he serves." One mysterious animal especially aroused his fascination: the otter. Inside its cage and surrounded by an artificial grotto, it swam in a dark pool and would dart occasionally to the surface. Walter would scan the water for it to appear: "If I finally succeeded it was certainly just for an instant, for in the blink of an eye the glistening inmate of the cistern would disappear once more into the wet night." In Walter's imagination, this magical scene became a microcosm for all of Berlin and the hidden passages by which its neighborhoods converged.

> When I gazed into the water, it always seemed as though the rain poured down into all the street drains of the city only to end up in this one basin and nourish its inhabitant. For this was the abode of a pampered animal whose empty, damp grotto was more a temple than a refuge. It was the sacred animal of the rainwater. But whether it was formed in this runoff of the rains, or only fed from arriving streams and rivulets, is something I could not have decided.[10]

The young Walter was not only entranced by the otter, he also identified with it. "The long, sweet day was never long, never sweeter, than when a fine- or thick-toothed drizzle slowly combed the animal for hours and minutes." The rain suited Walter's melancholy temper. "I heard it drumming on the windowpanes, streaming out of gutters, and rushing in a steady gurgle down the drainpipes. In a good rain, I was securely hidden away. And it would whisper to me of my future, as one sings a lullaby beside the cradle." When he returned to the otter's cage he would need to wait for a long while, until, finally, "the glistening black body darted up to the surface, only to hurry back almost immediately to urgent affairs below."[11]

In this innocent memory Benjamin conveys something essential about his habits of interpretation. In his writing nearly everything is transformed as if by magic into a metaphor for which only he possesses the key. Hidden passageways lead to submerged treasures that he then displays as priceless discoveries, as if they revealed all the secrets of the world. Many years later, this method would inspire his friend Hannah Arendt to describe him as a "pearl diver." Like his father the art dealer and auctioneer, Benjamin was by habit a collector. At first he collected stamps and butterflies, then children's toys and books; but he also collected quotations or brief insights that he transcribed for his work.[12] Many of these would serve as both the substance and architecture for his unfinished study of the Parisian arcades. "Nothing was more characteristic of him in the thirties," Arendt writes, "than the little notebooks with black covers which he always carried with him and in which he tirelessly entered in the form of quotations what daily living and reading netted him in the way of 'pearls' and 'coral.'"[13] Benjamin came to see history itself as a kind of ruin. During his many years in Paris as an independent scholar, he spent long hours in the Bibliothèque Nationale in order to fathom the secret meanings of the nineteenth century, a century that belonged not only to Charles Baudelaire and Marx and Pierre-Joseph Proudhon but also to his own parents. By diving into the wreck, he would bring this century alive and turn the bourgeois past into an empire of signs.

Judaism and Temptation

Whether it would be accurate to characterize Benjamin as a Jew will depend on complex definitions that, like much in Jewish history, are ever changing and seldom beyond dispute. In his childhood home, his mother Pauline subscribed to the customs of Reform Judaism that had first been codified by Abraham Geiger, who wished to revivify the Jewish faith by adapting it to the modern era. Following the model of liberal Protestantism that had emerged in nineteenth-century Germany, Geiger believed that modern Judaism had to accept the major lesson of Jewish historicist scholarship (as exemplified by the movement known as the *Wissenschaft des Judentums*). Judaism, for Geiger, was an evolving and *historical* faith: it was said to consist not in an adherence to *halacha* or orthodox law but in a principled commitment to a spiritual essence or "inner moral force."[14] Little of this doctrine, however, was passed down with any precision to the children in the Benjamin home. Of religious learning the young Walter received very little. He did not attend a Jewish religious school; he knew neither the Hebrew language nor the Talmud; and his observance of the major holidays was half-hearted and erratic.

Perhaps the most vivid illustration of this indifference to the Jewish religion is the early episode Benjamin relates in his *Berlin Childhood*, in a brief addendum to the original version of the text that bears the title "Sexual Awakening." It is admittedly a provocative passage, and maybe he *meant* it to provoke. The episode is one in which religious obligation competes with "the awakening of the sex drive (whose time had come)." Benjamin writes that the episode occurred when he was wandering through the Berlin streets at night. He adds that "it was the Jewish New Year, and my parents had arranged for me to be present at a ceremony of public worship." For this special occasion his parents had instructed him to visit a "distant relative" whose name is not mentioned but who had in his possession the admission tickets that would be necessary to enter the synagogue. Benjamin writes that he lost his way; he speculates that this may have been due to his unfavorable feelings toward this relative ("a virtual stranger") but also what he describes as a "suspicion of religious ceremonies, which promised only embarrassment." Although seized by dismay that he would never arrive at the synagogue on time, he also felt insouciant, perhaps even relieved. "And the

Young Walter as a child with his brother Georg and sister Dora, 1904

two waves converged irresistibly in a dawning sensation of pleasure, wherein the profanation of the holy day combined with the pandering of the street, which here, for the first time, gave me an inkling of the services it was prepared to render to awakened instincts."[15]

Whether Benjamin meant to include this section in the book's published version remains uncertain. His friend Gershom Scholem feared that it would provoke hatred or scandal, and advised him to delete it. He warned that "it was the only one in the whole book in which Jewish matters were explicitly mentioned, thus creating especially distorted associations." Scholem further explained that "There would have been no point in leaving out this section if his Jewish experiences had been voiced in other sections as well, but it would have been wrong to have kept it in this isolated position."[16] In a letter dated January 15, 1933, Benjamin responded that he felt Scholem's fears were justified and he would omit the offending passage. But their mutual friend Adorno did not know of this agreement, and so the episode appeared in the first edition of the complete text, which Adorno published in 1950. It reappeared verbatim in all subsequent editions.

How should we interpret this little misunderstanding? It was hardly uncommon for Scholem to feel concerned for his friend's reputation, but we cannot take Benjamin's consent to omit the passage as decisive. The fact that he wrote the section at all may imply at least a readiness to write for a public readership concerning matters about which he apparently felt little shame. We cannot tell from the passage whether his initial anxiety was due to a sense of genuinely religious obligation or only to the embarrassment of arriving late. A respectable congregation of Reform Jews in Berlin would likely expect a young man to show up on time. The episode suggests that the young Walter himself felt only a wave of "utter indifference." He dismisses any shame with an inward thought: "So be it—I don't care."[17]

But this gesture of dismissal is also a literary effect; it appears in a work he composed years later. We cannot know with any certainty whether literature reflects life. Did the young Walter actually experience two waves of feeling—the first religious, the second sexual? Did he mean to imply that he had left religious duties behind? Was this report a small act of heresy, a willful shift from the sacred to the profane? Or was it a confession that, in his imagination, religion and sexuality were somehow intertwined?

Such questions are not easily resolved. In any event, this was by no means the last time that Benjamin was confronted with the question of whether he felt any enduring commitment to the Jewish people or to Judaism. The general question of whether he belongs to a distinctive canon of Jewish thought—or even religious thought in general—raises a host of interpretive puzzles. Even today the question continues to provoke bitter feuds among scholars who wish to claim him for various causes. Many years later in his notes for *The Arcades Project*, Benjamin would try to explain to himself how he understood his odd habit of intermingling theological with secular themes. "My work," he writes, "is related to theology as blotting pad is related to ink. It is saturated with it. Were one to go by the blotter, however, nothing of what is written would remain." The analogy is curious, and like much of what Benjamin writes about theology or religion it resists any straightforward reading. If theology only plays the role of ink, then it is not quite the *source* of his thinking but only the *medium* in which he writes it down. Without the ink, however, he could not write at all. And yet, his thinking is meant to absorb theology, much like an ink blotter would absorb the ink; and it absorbs it so completely that any *overt* signs of theology are said to vanish. This is hardly the credo of a purely secular thinker; it takes instruction from theology but in the very same instant puts it to secular use. In a summary of his late friend's work, Adorno describe this act as a "migration into the profane."[18] Scholem, however, introduced a subtle modification: Benjamin, he claimed, was "a theologian *marooned* in the realm of the profane."[19]

The difference is not insignificant. The concept of migration suggests a gesture of borrowing or travel, as if one could cross a bridge from theological to secular realms. For Scholem this bridge is not secure: Benjamin appears not as a migrant but as a castaway who has lost all connection with the authentic sources of his thought. The debate between Adorno and Scholem is not easily resolved: was Benjamin more migrant or castaway? Mere facts of biography cannot answer the question. Yet the story of young Walter—losing his way to synagogue and finding himself in the most profane streets of Berlin—is suggestive not least because it implies feelings of both conflict *and* rebellion. Did he feel shame that he did not make it in time for religious services? Or was he proud to have strayed, perhaps because he assigned greater importance to purely carnal happiness? This question, troubling yet poignant, was to remain a constant theme even in his mature writing.

All the same, we should not neglect the sociological fact of his family's milieu. There is scant evidence that Benjamin ever felt a strong interest in adopting the actual practices of Judaism, such as the laws of kashrut or regular prayer. In the Berlin of his childhood, however, he found he was immersed in a thriving Jewish subculture even as he rebelled against it. When Walter was nine, Pauline and Emil determined that he should be enrolled in the Kaiser Friedrich School, a secondary school in Charlottenburg to which many of Berlin's well-to-do families sent their children. In the years before the First World War, official records from the school's director confirmed that more than a third of the students there were of Jewish descent. Hans Simmel, born in 1891, just one year after Walter, was the son of the esteemed sociologist Georg Simmel (a Jew by descent but whose parents were converts to Christianity).[20] Albert Salomon, also born in 1891, was a sociologist and later an editor of the Social Democratic journal *Die Gesellschaft;* following the Nazi seizure of power he fled to the United States where he taught at the New School for Social Research.

What this may tell us about Benjamin's own sense of being a Jew remains unclear. No doubt it would be hazardous to draw inferences from general statistics of group identity to the particular significance that this identity may hold for any single person. No individual is a mere exemplar of the social whole. Nevertheless, the high percentage of Jews in the Kaiser Friedrich School is noteworthy. In 1900 the total Jewish population of Berlin was estimated to be 92,000; the overall Berlin population at that time was approximately 1.88 million.[21] The Jewish community thus made up less than 5 percent of the city's total inhabitants, while Jewish students were more than 33 percent of the students at young Walter's school. So we can hardly find it surprising that many of his childhood classmates belonged to the same German-Jewish fold. Among his closer friends at the time were Franz Sachs (born in Berlin in 1894) and Herbert Blumenthal (born in 1893; later Herbert Belmore).[22] Although not all of these friendships would prove lasting, for Benjamin they set the pattern for habits of socialization and elective affinities that would endure throughout his life. This pattern also left an indelible mark on his work. Even if he was seldom preoccupied with explicitly Jewish themes, his thinking was like an ink blotter that had absorbed the ink of his tribe.

Scenes from Childhood

Despite its subtle inflections of Jewish identity, young Walter's experiences at the turn of the century were in many respects not unlike those of other children among the wealthier portions of the Berlin bourgeoisie. The family kept a second home outside the city limits, and they took vacations to places near and far, to the Baltic and the North Sea, to the Black Forest and Switzerland, and in the high mountains that lie north of Bohemia.[23] Even when he remained in Berlin, Walter found himself in the school library or at home, where he could immerse himself in stories of adventure set in exotic lands, in Babylon or Acre or Alaska. He also liked to paint in watercolors, and in his imagination the colors he mixed on the palette would become a disguise, coloring him as well. His mother had a large piece of jewelry that he found especially entrancing. "At its center was a large, sparkling yellow gem encircled by some even larger stones of various colors—green, blue, yellow, pink, purple." All of these, the vacations and the jewelry, belonged to the conventional arsenal by which the family deployed its wealth for both comfort and display. When the family entertained guests Walter might be permitted to assist in laying out utensils and glassware for the table: lobster forks and oyster knives, long-stemmed green wine-glasses, fine-cut little glasses for port, filigreed glasses for champagne, saltcellars made of silver, and carafe stoppers shaped like animals or gnomes.[24]

This was the bric-a-brac of abundance, the household's wealth growing with Emil's financial success. The Benjamins even had a French governess.[25] The family moved gradually westward into the greener and more prosperous portions of Berlin.[26] In 1912 they finally moved into a villa on Delbrückstrasse in the Grunewald on the city's westernmost outskirts—a location that brought an illusion of peace in the final years before the outbreak of war. Technology was already transforming both the cityscape and the family home. Sometime around the turn of the century, a telephone was installed in the hallway, though by this point the device was no longer a great novelty; in 1898 the subscription rate in Berlin had soared to an estimated 46,000 customers. But its arrival in the Benjamin household introduced "devastation." Its ring sounded like an alarm, shattering the peace of the parent's habitual afternoon nap. Walter recalled his father's strenuous efforts when cranking the handle, and his fear that the trembling employee on the other end of the line might suffer a stroke.[27] But among all of the objects in the Benjamin household the young Walter was especially drawn to a collection of Chinese porcelain—vases, plates, bowls, and boxes—none of which were of great value. They were "cheap export articles," but they nonetheless stirred his imagination. When painting with his watercolors he was reminded of the Chinese story of an old painter who invites friends to see his newest picture:

> This picture showed a park and a narrow footpath that ran along a stream through a grove of trees, culminating at a door of a little cottage in the background. When the painter's friends, however, looked around for the painter, they saw that he was gone—that he was in the picture. There, he followed the little path that led to the door, paused before it quite still, turned, smiled, and disappeared through the narrow opening.[28]

In his imagination the young Walter, much like the Chinese painter, merged with his work even to the point of disappearance. He loved to hide.

His parents made it possible for him to live in relative isolation from the darker realities of the city. He describes himself as a "prisoner" whose milieu was confined to the two districts of Berlin, the Old West and the New West. "They dwelt there in a frame of mind compounded of obstinacy and self-satisfaction, an attitude that transformed these neighborhoods into a ghetto." His life was sheltered, and he seldom encountered the poor directly; they existed mostly as nameless beggars whose lives were elsewhere. But what he did not actually know of urban poverty he tried to conjure in his imagination. In an early piece of fiction, he wrote of a poor man who distributes leaflets but suffers humiliation from "a public that has no interest in his literature." The cocoon-like safety of his early years was also secured by his schooling with private tutors. His parents did not entrust him to the Kaiser Friedrich School until he was almost nine. He had one teacher, Helene Pufahl, whom he admired before all others and whose name became a symbol of "lamblike piety and love of learning." On a signed postcard that he treasured as part of his collection, Benjamin imagined that her signature might have consisted in consonants alone, "like some Semitic text." Stripped to its essence, it would have been not only "the seat of calligraphic perfection" but also "the root of all virtues."[29]

But even the happiest of lives is exposed to intimations of death. When tragedy struck one of the pupils in his group, for Walter the event became a signpost at the boundary-line of his own childhood. In *A Berlin Childhood* he recalls that "Boys and girls from the better families of the bourgeois West took part in Fräulein Pufahl's circle. In certain cases one was not too particular, so that into this domain of the bourgeoisie a little girl of the nobility might also stray. She was called Luise von Landau, and the name soon had me under its spell." This unfortunate child died at a young age, though Walter had already left the enchanted circle and had joined the middle school:

> When I now passed by the banks of the Lützkov, I would always cast my eyes in the direction of her house. It lay, by chance, opposite a little garden that overhung the water on the other bank. And this garden plot I gradually wove together so intimately with the beloved name that I finally came to the conclusion that the flowerbed on the riverbank, so resplendent and inviolable, was the cenotaph of the departed child.[30]

In his memoir we do not learn how Luise might have died. Was it illness, or an accident? Did she drown? The flowers planted along the canal may have marked either the actual location of her death or only a peaceful spot for commemoration. But it is characteristic of Benjamin as a writer that, when he recalled the event later in life, he interlaced it with metaphors until it was transformed into literature. In much of his writing, water appears as a persistent symbol though its meanings are often uncertain: it is a surface in which one can discover one's own reflection but also a depth into which one can vanish. It is Lethe, the river of forgetting, but it is also Styx, the river that souls must cross as they pass onward to the underworld. It can signify imagination, hope, but also death. For Benjamin it also marked the end of childhood. "In those days," he recalls, "the shoreline of adult life appeared to me just as cut off from my own existence, by the river course of many years, as that bank of the canal on which the flowerbed lay."[31]

2

Youth and Utopia

In the decade preceding the First World War, from 1904 to 1914, Benjamin underwent a dramatic transformation, leaving behind the world of his childhood and embarking on the trials of adolescence and early maturity. In the fall of 1904, when he was only twelve, he was sent to a boarding school far from home; ten years later, when the war broke out, he had just turned twenty-two. In the intervening decade, he gradually awakened to questions of ideology and identity. What meaning, individual and collective, would he find in history? What meaning would he ascribe to his life as both a German and a Jew? To what career did he feel himself called? In his early correspondence, these questions emerged as major themes, and in his life he wrestled with them endlessly, turning his attention toward philosophy and literature. In 1913 he published a pseudonymous essay with the simple title "Experience." The essay ends with a line from

Nietzsche: "As Zarathustra says, the individual can experience himself only at the end of his wandering."[1]

Prophet of Youth

When their son Walter reached the age of twelve, Pauline and Emil withdrew him from the Kaiser Friedrich School and enrolled him in a boarding school in Haubinda. Located just south of the Thuringian forest in central Germany, Haubinda was only one example among the many experiments in educational reform that were sprouting up across Germany at that time. Introduced in 1898, the country boarding schools movement harbored a strong antipathy to political liberalism and urban life, and a no less passionate conviction that young boys could grow healthy and strong only if they were emancipated from the one-sided intellectualism of modern culture. The program at Haubinda nourished an attitude that one scholar has called "Spartan naturalism."[2] Young men were encouraged to feel unashamed of their nudity; they took cold showers, and the curriculum emphasized both practical skills as well as a canon of traditional book-learning tinged with German nationalism. The young Walter was not physically vigorous and was prone to illness. His parents hoped that the Haubinda school might restore him to greater health.

It should come as no surprise that the ethos of the country boarding schools at times carried at least a hint of anti-Semitism. In the decades that preceded the First World War, anxieties concerning the commercialism and intellectualism of modern city life coalesced into a loose constellation of values and motifs that (borrowing from the historian Shulamith Volkov) we might call "anti-Semitism as a cultural code."[3] In this respect the informal logic of anti-Semitism resembles other patterns of collective prejudice: it infuses both thought and action even if it does not always harden into explicit doctrine. In the popular imagination, group stereotypes or caricatures often ebb and flow without the least appearance of rational coherence or explicit argument, and this may help to explain why anti-Semitism persists in so many forms and often works its effects just below the threshold of consciousness. Even the victims of prejudice can internalize its themes and become the unwitting vehicles of its diffusion.

Such was the case with the youth movement, the fashionable wave that swept through Germany and helped to inspire the country boarding schools. Officially founded in 1896, the youth movement, often known by a more poetic name, the *Wandervogel*, was never a single organization; it was merely a collective name for the broad spectrum of clubs and societies that flourished during the first decades of the twentieth century, uniting both young men and women with the promise of cultural and spiritual renewal.[4] Common to all of these movements was a general sentiment that the youth must turn back to nature to regain the vitality and sense of purpose that modern civilization threatened to destroy. True to their name, flocks of students took up the movement's typical rituals, such as hiking in the forests and singing as they marched along. The youth movement branched out into a remarkable diversity of groups that embraced ideologies spanning the political spectrum—from German nationalism and pacifism to socialism and Zionism.

The Free School Movement was founded at the turn of the century by a teacher, Hermann Leitz, in close alliance with the youth movement, and it soon branched out into several schools, including the Wickersdorf Free School Community at Haubinda. Walter felt especially drawn to Gustav Wyneken, the director, who had been appointed to the school only the previous year.[5] A sagelike and charismatic figure in the youth movement, Wyneken was first and foremost a gifted teacher whose ideas consisted in a powerful brew of Hegelian and Nietzschean themes. He remained an important inspiration for Walter right up to the outbreak of the First World War, when Wyneken's decision to embrace the German war effort caused a permanent rupture in their friendship. Wyneken himself was by no means anti-Semitic, and he felt no compunctions about admitting Jewish students to his school. The case of Leitz, however, is considerably less clear. Leitz was willing to admit young men like Walter who came from the wealthier and more assimilated stratum of German Jewry. But he had created the Free School Movement with the express purpose of educating a new generation of youth in accordance with the values of the youth movement, or *Jugendbewegung*, and he did not wish to see his utopian dream compromised. As an institution Wickersdorf was not particularly inclined to German nationalism, and Jewish students were not unwelcome; in one class they even made up a majority.[6] All the same, when the young Walter arrived at Wickersdorf in 1904, an unpleasant memory of anti-Semitism still lingered in the air.

The controversy had erupted at the school a year earlier, in 1903, when Theodor Lessing was appointed as an instructor.[7] Lessing, a German-Jewish philosopher and public intellectual well known for his acerbic style, had first come to Haubinda at Leitz's invitation. But the two men soon found themselves at odds. Leitz was an unapologetic German nationalist who considered the presence of Jewish students tolerable at best. Lessing, though no less devoted to the movement for school reform, felt that it must be cleansed of its anti-modernist chauvinism. In a public statement he faulted the movement for its "anti-cultural rusticity."[8] Lessing was then dismissed from his post, and from that point forward Leitz adopted the policy that Jewish students should be admitted only on an exceptional basis. In the coming years Lessing would emerge as an advocate for pacifism and a fierce critic of German conservative politics; even today, his book *Jewish Self-Hatred* (1930) still arouses debate.[9] In 1933 he was assassinated in Czechoslovakia by Sudetenland Germans.

Lessing's dismissal from Haubinda aroused concern and rumors of anti-Semitism. But the memory of the Haubinda "Jewish dispute" did not dissuade Walter's parents from the decision to enroll him at Wickersdorf, and the young man's admiration for Gustav Wyneken grew only more pronounced from 1904 on. For a student who had spent his childhood surrounded by all the comforts of an urban home, the youth movement and its educational mission held out the promise of spiritual transformation. Like so many other students of his generation, the very idea of *youth* itself grew into a powerful (if politically ambiguous) symbol for renewal, a vision that inspired Germans and German Jews alike. Among his Jewish friends, some would turn to Zionism in search of the same utopian promise that Benjamin found at Wickersdorf. Zionism, too, after all, seemed to hold out for German Jewish youth the promise of political and cultural regeneration. Although Benjamin seldom expressed any deep attachment to Zionism as a practical political program, his attraction to the youth movement was sign of a similar longing for radical change. Especially for assimilated Jews, both movements nourished the hope that they might undergo a personal and spiritual metamorphosis, purging themselves of the qualities—of homelessness or deracination—that the ambient culture condemned. To condemn this longing for regeneration as a symptom of "self-hatred" would be unfair, but neither should we ignore the irony that such movements are seldom free of the prejudices they seek to overcome.[10]

From his studies with Wyneken the young Walter discovered a deep love of literature and poetry, and he even composed poems of his own. The earliest poem by Benjamin that we know of dates from around 1910 and does not carry the author's own name. Published in *Der Anfang*, a student journal, he signed it with a pseudonym, "Ardor," and he gave it a simple title: "Der Dichter" ("The Poet"). Written in a highly Romantic style that plunders shamelessly from Greek mythology, it is no doubt a work of juvenilia:

> Assembled around the throne of Zeus there stood
> The Olympian gods. And Apollo spoke:
> Directing his questioning gaze toward Zeus:
> "Great Zeus, in your powerful creation
> I can recognize every member,
> As it stands out in sharp vision from the others
> Only the poet do I seek in vain."

Zeus then responds to Apollo, and instructs him to look down upon humanity in all its variety. Below Apollo sees how some walk in silence down the street, their empty gaze turned to the ground. But among them he also finds one individual who is "standing without care between black night and colorful life."

> This one stands in unchanging calm
> Solitary, standing back from the stream of life.
> At times casting his deep gaze within himself,
> At times bravely look in the light upward to us,
> At times, too, casting his great look upon the multitude.
> His pen writes down lines of verse.—
> Look upon this one and know—he is the poet.[11]

It demands little effort to read this poem as a self-portrait: the "poet," it would seem, is Benjamin himself, solitary, reserved, and given to introspection. The poet refuses to plunge into the anonymity of the crowd: the word *Menge* (translated here as "multitude") underscores the distinction between the individual and the quotidian masses. The poet possesses both courage and calm: by setting himself apart from the crowd he can also know the gods above. Even the charitable reader will likely admit that the poem is little more than a symptom of adolescent immodesty. But it also bespeaks a quasi-religious devotion to work which, in the coming years, may prove even stronger than a devotion to life itself.

The German-Jewish Parnassus

In March 1912, a young journalist named Moritz Goldstein published a provocative essay with the title "The German-Jewish Parnassus." The essay appeared in *Der Kunstwart*, a highly esteemed and politically conservative journal for the arts that was known for its nationalist and occasionally anti-Semitic tendencies.[12] Goldstein had first submitted the essay to the *Berliner Tageblatt*, a politically liberal paper whose owner, Hans Lachmann-Mosse, was a scion of the Mosse family, a Jewish family that had risen to wealth and prominence in the world of German publishing. Due to the explosive nature of its claims, however, Goldstein's essay had been rejected. Its author then submitted it to *Der Kunstwart*, whose editors decided to print it but appended a brief prefatory note: They felt obliged to explain that the essay did not represent the official opinion of the journal, though they hoped that it might serve as a starting point for further discussion. It would, they predicted, "cause a sensation among Jews and non-Jews alike."

The essay did just that. It raised a series of uncomfortable questions about the prominent place of Jews in German culture. At the time Goldstein considered himself a committed Zionist, and he believed that Jews must fashion an autonomous culture for themselves. His essay was a warning: over the century of gradual emancipation, German Jews had neglected their own cultural efforts while achieving a disproportionate influence in German culture. "Whenever they were allowed access, they were up to the task. Yes, due to some mysterious qualities, they showed themselves to be the superior ones: despite their small number, despite all the difficulties they had to overcome on their way, they outstripped their teachers." In whatever domain they were permitted entry and not repelled by force, they became the custodians of a German culture that was not truly theirs. Over time it even seemed that German cultural life might gradually "pass into Jewish hands." But their presence was not altogether welcome. Their Christian hosts had begun to resist and once again raised the cry that the Jews were foreign agents who would desecrate their temple. The Jewish population was now confronted with a grave dilemma: "We Jews," Goldstein wrote, "manage the intellectual property of a people that denies us the right and the ability to do so."

Goldstein's arguments proved highly provocative, and Benjamin was only one individual among many who were drawn into the debate. Beginning in mid-September 1912, he argued over the essay with Ludwig Strauss, a close friend and a committed Zionist who would later emigrate to Israel. In a candid exchange of letters that extended over the course of several months, Benjamin and Strauss debated the merits of the essay and the many questions it raised. Benjamin had just returned from a two-week vacation on the Baltic coast, where he had also discussed the essay with some acquaintances who (as he noted to Strauss) were also Zionist in their political orientation. Unfortunately, the full set of letters from Strauss himself has not been preserved. But some sense of his opinions can be gleaned from his own anonymous contribution to the debate (also published in *Der Kunstwart* in August 1912) and from Benjamin's own side of the exchange.[13] To Strauss it was obvious that the essay had considerable merit. "In the Zionist movement," he wrote, "the thought of national regeneration is thrust ever more to the fore. . . . Today, many German Jews struggle for an assimilation that the greater share of them have failed. . . . What has emerged are hermaphrodites [*Zwittermenschen*] and a neutered culture imbued with the innermost uncertainty." For this condition Strauss saw only one true remedy. It would be necessary to establish a "focal point" for the "spiritual life" of the Jewish people. "Our most important assignment is to root the rootless Jewry of Germany once again in the ground of the Jewish spirit." To achieve this task, "the national-Jewish movement in

Germany" would be obliged, sooner or later, to direct all of its power to "the diffusion of the Hebrew language, for it alone is capable of bringing our Jewry to its full realization."[14]

In the ensuing correspondence between Benjamin and Strauss, their differences soon became apparent, and Benjamin was compelled to reckon, more than he ever had before, with the question of whether he ascribed any particular meaning to his own identity as a Jew. His answers suggest a mixture of feelings, ambivalence but also regret. He agreed with Goldstein's arguments, at least in part, and he seemed ready to embrace Strauss's proposal that Jews should forge a culture of their own. "If we are two-sided, Jewish and German," Benjamin wrote, "we have indeed until now oriented ourselves with all of our affirmation toward the German side; in our productivity and in our life the Jewish aspect was, perhaps, often only a foreign land, a southern (or worse, sentimental) aroma." Benjamin admitted that there was some truth in what his friend Strauss had said. "Until now," he allowed, German Jewry has permitted itself to see the world "with German eyes." He also welcomed Strauss's plan to inaugurate a new journal for "Jewish intellectual life in the German language [*Jüdisches Geistesleben in deutscher Sprache*]."[15]

But these words of agreement were interlaced with ambivalence. Notwithstanding his enthusiasm for the idea of a new journal on Jewish intellectual culture in Germany, Benjamin was quick to disagree with Strauss regarding the importance of political Zionism. He was willing to allow that Zionism may be of importance for "eastern European Jewry," and that perhaps their only salvation would be found in a Jewish state. But he believed that for western European Jewry the future lies along a different path. Unlike their impoverished co-religionists in the east, Jews in western Europe could and should not confine themselves to an exclusively nationalist and statist project. Why, Benjamin asked, should the Jews in the western European sphere not feel themselves free to realize their self-consciousness in a "*cultural state* [*Kulturstaat*]?"[16] The cultural ideal of western European Jewry was untethered from political Zionism or any other political nationalism. "In both their being and their will, [western European] Jews . . . are leading figures in the sciences, literature, and commerce," and they must therefore adhere to "internationalism." To justify his opinion Benjamin invoked the favorable phrases of the left-liberal novelist Heinrich Mann, who had recently affirmed the vital role that Jews played in European culture. "What," Mann had asked, "would become of spirit, art, and love among us without the Jews?"[17]

The correspondence with Strauss is revealing. The young Benjamin, now twenty years old, assigns his Jewish identity an extraordinary importance, and on this point, at least, he finds himself in agreement with Strauss. "That the Jewish is *essential*—this is also my view . . . as it has developed in the last months."[18] But when the topic turns to Zionism they reach an impasse. To the question of "whether my stand toward Zionism is one of unconditional affirmation," Benjamin cannot agree. "No," he responds, "for me matters are not so simple." "In light of what has already been said it's a given that I recognize Zionism, and in a certain way support it, i.e., I would pay a contribution to a German Zionist organization." His supportive stand toward Zionism may reflect his conversations earlier that summer with young partisans of the *Blau-Weiss* group, the largest organization for Zionist youth, which was founded in 1912. Benjamin, however, does not feel that his principled support for Zionism truly captures his own personal orientation. "Zionism does not define me," he explains, "even while I said before that I feel Judaism [*Judentum*] as the core of my being. For modern west European national Jewry I see two paths: Zionism and one other. It is possible that, when I make you understand this path and the necessity that leads me to it, we will greet each other in surprise as fellow travelers."[19]

Benjamin explains that his most decisive spiritual experience came to him well before Judaism [*das Judentum*] ever arose as a personal question. He was raised as a "liberal" (by which he presumably means as a political liberal and not according to the tenets of liberal or Reform Judaism). What he knew of Judaism itself, however, was "in actuality only anti-Semitism and an indeterminate piety." As a religion, Judaism remained "distant," while "as a national matter" it was wholly unknown. What Benjamin calls "the most decisive influence" was the period (lasting less than two years) that he had spent in the country boarding school in Wickersdorf, where he had received instruction from Gustav Wyneken. It was not Judaism itself but rather Wyneken's teaching, with its torrent of Hegelian and Nietzschean themes, that left the strongest impression on Benjamin and those from his Berlin milieu.[20] "I see in Wickersdorf," Benjamin writes, "something that has had the innermost influence on me and on other Jews." He remains bound, both body and soul, to what he calls the "Wickersdorf *Idea*," and abandoning that idea is virtually unthinkable. "Only *one* idea can prevail," he explains, and "every other idea must submit itself to the test, the Jewish too." Notwithstanding this declaration of unwavering fidelity to Wickersdorf, he feels no inner conflict between the two commitments. Although he is and will remain "a strong and fanatical student of G. Wyneken," it is through his experiences at Wickersdorf that he has also discovered what he simply calls "*my Judaism*."[21]

The exchange with Strauss shows us that Benjamin remains in his heart both Jewish *and* European. He identifies three strands among Zionist Jewry: Palestinian Zionism (which he calls a "necessity of nature"); German Zionism (which he sees as a "half-measure"); and cultural Zionism (which works for "Jewish values *in all places*"). Of these three possibilities he identifies himself only with the third, the idea of cultural Zionism as elaborated by the Hebrew essayist Ahad Ha'am.[22] He affirms that for Jews who are threatened, conditions for their existence in Palestine "should and must be created." But even if he can feel sympathy with Zionism as an idea he cannot adopt it as his own "political imperative." This is chiefly because he sees in politics only "the choice of the lesser evil." The cold realism that prevails in politics does not honor the cultural ideals that he cherishes most of all. Such ideals are far too expansive for a nationalistic and *political* movement, even if they do permit him feelings of cultural pride. He declares that "my experience has brought me to the insight that among the ranks of the intellectuals Jews constitute an elite." All the same, he takes care to explain that he does not identify himself with any specific political orientation. Whether he counts himself a member of what he describes as "left-liberalism" or locates himself on "the social-democratic wing" remains uncertain. In any event, he knows that Jews must sustain their leading role as representatives of cosmopolitan ideals in European culture. "For me it is idle to ask the question whether Jewish work in Palestine or Jewish work in Europe is more urgent. I am bound here."[23]

I am bound here. The phrase may strike us as rich in irony, since in the coming years Benjamin would become a peripatetic, a wanderer who shifted from one city to another. Yet over the course of his life his convictions on the question of Jewish identity seldom wavered, even if he came to recognize (too late) that his own embattled position in Europe was no longer safe and that he was compelled, against his will, to seek a home elsewhere, in the United States or perhaps even in Palestine. All the same, exigencies cannot be confused with ideals. In his heart Benjamin would remain, always and incorrigibly, a European Jew.

Café of Grand Illusions

In 1912 the young man commenced his academic studies at the Albert Ludwig University in Freiburg, where he took courses in literature, history, and philosophy. To his friend Herbert Belmore he describes the view from his window: "The church square with a tall poplar (the yellow sun in its green foliage) and in front of that an old fountain and the sun-drenched walls of the houses—I can stare at this for fifteen minutes at a time. Then—as you might expect, I lie down on the sofa for a while and pick up a volume of Goethe. As soon as I come upon a phrase like, 'the breadth of the divinity,' I have already lost control again."[24] In his first semester at Freiburg he enrolled in a course on epistemology and metaphysics taught by Heinrich Rickert, one of the most esteemed philosophers in all of Germany, known chiefly for his contributions to the neo-Kantian movement. Among the students in the same course was the young Martin Heidegger, who was just three years older than Benjamin but would emerge by the later 1920s as one of the most consequential philosophers of the century. In later semesters, Benjamin would plunge deeper into philosophical works such as Immanuel Kant's *Prolegomena to any Future Metaphysics*, and Søren Kierkegaard's *Either/Or*. Meanwhile he continued his work for the youth movement, and he wrote a rhapsodic essay with the title "The Metaphysics of Youth," in which he poured out a welter of speculative thoughts on love, silence, and time:

> We wish to pay heed to the sources of the unnamable despair that flows in every soul. The souls listen expectantly to the melody of their youth—a youth that is guaranteed them a thousandfold. But the more they immerse themselves in the uncertain decades and broach that part of their youth which is most laden with future, the more orphaned they are in the emptiness of the present.[25]

The Romantic spirit that courses through this early essay also appears in an early essay on the poet Friedrich Hölderlin; it later inspired the doctoral dissertation on the concept of criticism in German Romanticism. During his second semester at Freiburg, Benjamin also made the acquaintance of a young man named Fritz Heinle, whose poems moved him deeply. In a letter to Carla Seligson, another member of the youth movement (who later married his friend Herbert Belmore), he writes that he and Heinle swiftly became close friends. Soon they were taking long walks together in the Black Forest, staying out well past midnight, sharing their passion for the youth movement and for the ideals of educational reform.[26]

In the summer of 1914 Benjamin passed much of his time with students and friends at the Café des Westens, a popular spot on the Kurfürstendamm. Nicknamed by Berliners with characteristic irony as the "Café Grössenwahn," or café of grand delusion, it became a favorite gathering place for left-wing artists and bohemians, including Erich Mühsam and Else Lasker-Schüler, both of them Jewish and both accomplished poets.[27] Mühsam, an anarchist and fierce opponent of German militarism, would later emerge as a leading figure in the Bavarian Socialist Republic; when the Nazis took over they exacted a swift revenge: he was tortured and killed in 1934. Lasker-Schüler, became one of the foremost representatives of German expressionist poetry; when the Nazis came to power she emigrated, first to Zürich and later to Palestine, a refuge that was not quite a home. Personally isolated and at times mocked by children, she became a fixture in a small Jerusalem café where (in the words of the poet Lea Goldberg) she "sat in her usual place, gray as a bat, small, poor, withdrawn."[28] In retrospect we can see the Café des Westens as a symbolic crossroads: gathered together in this one location were three individuals—a cultural critic, a revolutionary, a poet in exile. It was a point of momentary convergence for Jewish lives that would turn out very differently.[29]

Conscience and Catastrophe

War broke out in the summer of 1914. With friends there was some discussion as to how they might strategize in order to secure posts together; but for Benjamin himself it seemed that there was scant danger that he would see combat. With one glance, the examining doctor concluded that Walter's physical condition disqualified him for military duty.[30] His younger brother Georg was sent instead. On the 8th of August 1914, however, Benjamin experienced a personal tragedy that left him deeply shaken. His close friend Fritz Heinle, together with his fiancée Rika Seligson (Carla Seligson's sister), committed suicide. Whether they had made this choice as a love pact or as a protest against the coming war remains unclear, but Benjamin and those in his circle took the event as a further sign that the world was desperately out of joint.[31] Wracked with grief, he wrote a collection of sonnets, more than fifty in all, for his late friend.

The mobilization of the German military also brought about a permanent rupture in his personal relations with Wyneken, the leader of the youth movement to whom Benjamin had once entrusted his heart and soul. On November 25, 1914, Wyneken gave a public address in Munich, "War and Youth," in which he called upon his followers to dedicate themselves without restraint to the fatherland and its "*holy* cause."[32] For Benjamin the speech was an outrage. On March 9, 1915, he wrote a letter to Wyneken in which he accused his mentor of betraying the ideals he had once served. "You have sacrificed young people to the state," he wrote, adding: "The young, however, belong only to those with vision who love them and the *idea* in them above all. The idea has slipped out of your erring hands and will continue to suffer unspeakably." The letter is remarkable both for its political anger and its sense of personal betrayal. Benjamin explains that "it would be totally impossible for me to say a single word to the person who wrote those lines about the war and youth." His verdict is irrevocable: "I do not want to speak to you." He signed the letter without a valediction, as if it were a public notice.[33]

This letter is instructive not simply as a testament to Benjamin's opposition to the war. More important, it signifies an enduring strain of political idealism in his thinking that would persist even as he lost his enthusiasm for the youth movement and withdrew from active participation in its affairs. In an essay titled "The Life of Students" (published in 1915), he condemns the "complete assimilation of academic institutions to bourgeois conditions," and he laments that, as a community, today's students are "incapable of even formulating the issue of the role of learning or grasping its indissoluble protest against the vocational demands of the age." Students must resist what he calls "the secret tyranny of vocational training," for in student life what he finds of greatest value is that one possesses "the will to submit to a principle, to identify completely with an idea." The students must embody a "creative spirit," a "sense of infinity," and a "concern for humanity as a whole." The university, he adds, is more than an institution; it is a "metaphor" and "an image of the highest metaphysical state of history."

This essay stands as one of Benjamin's final statements on the youth movement, but it also marks a transition to loftier themes. For the students, he writes, have a "historical task" that cannot be confined to the university alone. Like "the utopian images of the philosophers," their goal points to something higher, "the idea of the French Revolution" or even "the messianic realm." In the coming years, embittered by Wyneken's betrayal and the horrors of the war itself, Benjamin's enthusiasm for the youth movement would dwindle away. But the utopian passion that had once been set aflame for "the metaphysics of youth" was not wholly extinguished. It burned with new ardor for different questions of philosophy and cultural criticism.[34]

3

From War to Peace

In the spring of 1915, Benjamin, twenty-two years old, heard a lecture in Berlin by Kurt Hiller, a socialist and pacifist who would later emerge as a vocal champion for gay rights.[1] In the lecture, "The Nature of the Historical Process," Hiller expounded a rich infusion of Nietzschean ideas, condemning history while praising "spirit" and "life." In the audience was a young man, Gerhard (later known by the Hebrew name Gershom) Scholem. Born in Berlin into an assimilated Jewish family, Scholem was then in his first semester at the university, where he pursued mathematics and philosophy, while also devoting time to studies of the Hebrew language and Jewish historical texts.[2] Scholem later confided to his diary that he found Hiller's argument "totally inadequate and wrongheaded."[3]

When the lecture concluded, there came an announcement: a group discussion of Hiller's arguments would convene in Charlottenburg a few days later. Scholem attended the discussion, where he began to criticize Hiller for his faulty remarks on history only to be cut short. Benjamin was also there and participated in the debate, though it seems that the two students had no direct contact during the meeting. This was not, however, the first time that Scholem had seen Benjamin in person. Before the war, in 1913, he had observed Benjamin at a meeting in the Tiergarten, where members of Jung Juda, the Zionist youth organization, had convened with followers of Wyneken (most of whom, Scholem recalled, were also Jewish). Although Benjamin had been appointed the chief speaker for Wyneken's group, Scholem saw that Benjamin wholly lacked the skills for the task: "Without looking at the audience, he delivered his absolutely letter-perfect speech with great intensity to an upper corner of the ceiling, at which he stared the whole time."[4]

A few days after the discussion in Charlottenburg, Benjamin and Scholem encountered each other once again, this time in the catalogue room at the university library. Benjamin, as always, was shy and impeccably polite. Through his thick glasses he appeared uncertain whether he knew who Scholem was. He left the room, then returned and (in Scholem's recollection) "made a perfect bow." He then inquired if Scholem was "the gentleman who had spoken at the Hiller discussion." Benjamin proposed that they meet on some evening later that week to discuss the themes of Hiller's speech in further detail. He invited Scholem to his family home on Delbrückstrasse, where Scholem was delighted to see that Benjamin had "a large, very respectable room with many books, which struck me as a philosopher's den." They plunged into a conversation that lasted more than three hours.[5]

Over the coming years the friendship between Benjamin and Scholem would grow in depth. Among other passions they shared a love of chess and played often. In mid-October 1915, Benjamin once again sought to secure a military deferment, and he asked that Scholem assist him in his plan. Meeting at the

Café des Westens, they then retired to Delbrückstrasse, where they played chess and chatted at length, from nine in the evening until six in the morning, while Benjamin drank great volumes of coffee, enough to leave him trembling. Later that day, the doctor who examined him for his physical was left convinced that the candidate was in poor health and perhaps even suffered from palsy. Benjamin received a deferment for another year.[6] Meanwhile, the friends conferred and conspired, finding in one another a true intellectual kinship despite occasional disagreements. Their sharpest point of dispute concerned Zionism. Benjamin continued to look upon the movement with skepticism, while Scholem embraced it without reservation. This was and would remain a matter of sharp disagreement that tested the bond between them. Yet Scholem's admiration for Benjamin was profound and verged at times on infatuation. To his diary in 1917, Scholem confided his true feelings: "In grasping what Benjamin has to say, the same astounding thing always happens to me: at first I'm standing somewhere on the wide earth while Benjamin's in heaven. Then what is said comes closer to me, and suddenly I am in the center. Each time I feel the exact same instantaneous jolt."[7]

About one matter the friends found themselves in perfect accord. Both felt a strong allergy to Martin Buber, whose popular collection of Hasidic tales, published in the first decade of the twentieth century, had catapulted him to prominence in the renaissance of Jewish culture in Germany.[8] Chiefly thanks to his *Three Addresses on Judaism* (1911), Buber had also emerged as a leading advocate for Zionism, which he saw not as merely a political campaign but as a movement for spiritual renewal. Despite their different attitudes toward Zionism, neither Scholem nor Benjamin could muster much enthusiasm for Buber, whose neo-romantic mannerisms ill-suited their more restrained and intellectual tastes. In 1916 Buber founded a monthly journal, *Der Jude*, and soon after the publication of the first issue he invited Benjamin to contribute an essay. But Benjamin could not overcome his misgivings. He was especially piqued at the essay by the philosopher Hugo Bergmann, "Jewish Nationalism After the War," and the grandiose tone of Buber's own opening essay, "The Solution."[9] Buber had written that the Jews in wartime would harken to "the call of the deep community of blood." And he added: "Anyone who wants to be serious about their existence on earth must be serious about their relationship to the community; for to the community he feels his responsibility. Among the Jews who are shaken by the Jewish lived experience [*das jüdische Erlebnis*] of this war, among those who feel responsible for the fate of their community, there appears a new unity among Jews."[10]

For a student such as Benjamin who embraced a more cosmopolitan vision, Buber's heavy-handed nationalism seemed outrageous. But he was also repelled by Buber's typically florid and vitalist language. Benjamin intended to write an open letter in response, turning down the invitation to contribute and explaining in strong terms why he objected to the journal's ideological postures. Before doing so, however, he felt that it might be best to consult Scholem for guidance. His deliberations took nearly two months. In July 1916, he finally wrote his open letter to Buber in a tone that was more restrained, though his message was still clear. Although Benjamin confessed that he disagreed "intensely" with the contributions of the first volume, "especially their position on the European war," he explained that his objections to the journal were animated most of all by a theory of language. Language and political action, he wrote, cannot be disentangled. "Every action that derives from the expansive tendency to string words together seems terrible to me, and even more catastrophic where the entire relationship between word and deed is, to an ever-increasing degree, gaining ground as a mechanism for the realization of the true absolute."[11]

Most of all, Benjamin objected to the way in which Buber

employed language chiefly to mystify rather than to clarify and change political reality. "The crystal-pure elimination of the ineffable in language," Benjamin wrote, "is the most obvious form given to us to be effective within language." He did not deny that poetic language and prophecy have a legitimate role to play in opening the way toward religion. For *Der Jude*, however, such language was altogether inappropriate. "For a journal, the language of the poets, of the prophets, or even of those in power does not come into question. Neither do song, psalm, and imperative, which . . . may have totally different relationships to the ineffable and may be the source of an entirely different magic." A journal that means to address politics should not indulge in a language of religious mystification. "The only thing at issue is objective writing."[12]

It should be noted that Benjamin's strong distaste for Buber and his journal did not signal a lack of interest in Judaism itself. It was Scholem's impression at the time that Benjamin disliked the way in which the journal took the Zionist orientation as given and pursued its political mission without restraint, while wholly disregarding "the substance of Judaism," namely, "the Torah, the Talmud, and the Prophets."[13] Buber and his circle were also consumed with (in Scholem's words) the "cult of experience [*Erlebnis*]," a term that came enwreathed with magical power especially in Buber's early writing. *Erlebnisphilosophie*, or the philosophy of lived experience, was no doubt a fashion of the times.[14] But for a student educated in philosophy like Benjamin, the idea of lived or unmediated experience betrayed an intolerable species of irrationalism. Benjamin remarked to Scholem that Buber seemed as if he were "a man who lived in a permanent trance."[15]

The quarrel with Buber also reflects Benjamin's acute sensitivity to problems of language. At the time Benjamin was deepening his interest in German Romanticism, and he found himself especially drawn to Romantic critics such as Friedrich

Schlegel, whose speculations on language and art would furnish the topic of his doctoral dissertation. In 1916 he wrote an essay, "On Language as Such and the Language of Man," which marks a first, tentative foray into themes that would preoccupy him for the remainder of his life. In this essay he assigns an extraordinary importance to language: it does not merely consist in the medium of words; rather, language signifies expression in the broadest sense. In the state of paradise there existed only one language, by which each and every thing was endowed by God with the absolute singularity of a proper name. "For in his creative word, God called them into being, calling them by their proper names." After the fall, however, nature itself was stripped of its identity. It now suffers from "muteness" and "melancholy," and if it were somehow granted the gift of language it would only begin to lament. Unlike the divine language, in human language there emerges a multiplicity of names, no one of which expresses the essence of the thing. In the language of humankind, the name has "withered" and things are "overnamed." Yet even in postlapsarian nature there persists "a nameless, unspoken language," or what Benjamin calls "the residue of the creative word of God."[16]

Several themes in the language essay merit attention. Language assumes a primacy in Benjamin's thought that reaches beyond the narrow principles of any linguistic formalism or human communication: it means nothing less than the expressive web by which the world gains its intelligibility. With this theory, the conventional distinction between cultural meaning on one hand and brute nature on the other seems to collapse; although nature may suffer in relative silence, it retains just enough of its divine origin that it holds out the promise that one day it might speak. A few years later, especially in the study of German tragic drama, this theme would bear its greatest fruit when Benjamin struck upon his idea of *Naturgeschichte*, or "natural history."[17] Both nature and history appear as a realm that has fallen into decay and that awaits the grace of divine redemption. Closely related to this is the nominalist idea that each and every thing, both human and natural, possesses the singularity of a proper name.[18] This special theme reached its deepest elaboration in the early 1930s in the essay on mimesis, which Benjamin defined as a capacity to experience "non-sensuous similarity," whether it is discovered in magic or in the stars.[19]

Most of all, however, the essay on language marked a decisive turn to themes of religion, even if it did not mark an awakening to religious belief. Thanks chiefly to Scholem's influence, Benjamin began at this point to grapple more deeply with Judaism, not as a faith or devotional practice but as a conceptual inheritance. "If I ever have a philosophy of my own," he told Scholem, "it somehow will be a philosophy of Judaism."[20] A philosophy of religion, however, should not be equated with religious faith. The essay on language may be steeped in religious imagery, but it does not seek to unlock the secrets of the divine itself. Many years later, Benjamin wrote that "we have been endowed with a weak messianic power."[21] This theme of a religious *inheritance*, bequeathed to human beings and transformed in human hands, is already prefigured in the essay on language. The task of naming and knowing the things of this world is something that God assigns to humankind alone:

> In receiving the unspoken nameless language of things and converting it by name into sounds, man performs this task. It would be insoluble, were not the name-language of man and the nameless language of things related in God and released from the same creative word, which in things became the communication of matter in magic communion, and in man the language of knowledge and name in blissful mind.[22]

We should also note that Benjamin turned toward religion in general, not Judaism in particular. Although Scholem seemed eager to claim his friend as a thinker who belonged chiefly or even exclusively to the Jewish fold, Benjamin's intellectual curiosity was aroused not only by Judaism but by Christianity as well. This ecumenical sensibility became especially evident in "On the Program of the Coming Philosophy," an ambitious sketch from 1918 in which Benjamin entertained "the virtual unity of religion and philosophy." It is telling that, in this essay at least, the meaning of religion remains as broad and indefinite as the meaning of philosophy. Intellectually restless and impatient with the borderlines that conventionally distinguish one religion from another, he did not care to specify the doctrinal identity of the religion in question.[23]

Roses and Romance

Religion demands a singular devotion. *Thou shalt have no other gods before me.* But elevating one god above all others was not Benjamin's way. In matters of the heart, too, Benjamin seldom if ever found what he was seeking. In 1914 he became engaged to Grete Radt, the sister of his friend Fritz. A student at the time, Grete Radt was also active in the youth movement and had already contributed to *Der Anfang*, a journal of the youth movement for which Wyneken served as editor.[24] But the engagement with Radt did not last long. The truth is that Benjamin was better at longing than commitment. In early 1915 he had written an essay titled "The Rainbow," which he dedicated to Grete.[25] Although the essay is constructed as a philosophical conversation about color and the imagination, it is hard to suppress the thought that Benjamin had also discovered the perfect metaphor for his romantic life: chasing after rainbows. Throughout his life this was his typical pattern: first seized by infatuation, he would collapse in bitter disappointment when his advances were rebuffed.

His troubled marriage to Dora Kellner may illustrate the point. Born in 1890, Dora belonged to a circle of Jewish intellectuals in Vienna. Her father, Leon Kellner, was a lecturer in English literature at the University of Vienna and also a close friend of Theodor Herzl; he had edited a collection of Herzl's writings on Zionism and even wrote a biography of Herzl, although he completed only the first volume of two.[26] Dora herself would later become a novelist and journalist. She worked in Berlin for the prestigious magazine *Die Literarische Welt*, among others, and she also translated many novels from English.[27] She had first encountered Benjamin in May 1914, when he delivered his speech as the newly elected chairperson of the Berlin Free Students' Union. When his speech was concluded, Dora gave him roses that his beloved Grete had sent along to congratulate him since she could not be there herself. To his friend Herbert Belmore he confided that "flowers have never made me as happy as these."[28] At the time Dora was already married to the journalist Max Pollack, but this did little to deter the growing feelings of affection between her and Walter. Affection soon blossomed into romance, and although Walter himself was engaged to Grete, their engagement did not last. By April 1917 Dora had separated from Pollack, and she and Walter were married.

Most reports suggest that their union was not a happy one, though Dora would remain an emotional and financial anchor for Benjamin well after their marriage had collapsed. In the summer of 1917 the couple fled together to Zurich, in part to evade Walter's military service. After several deferrals, the German army had determined that Benjamin was "fit for light field operations."[29] The move to Switzerland also brought a shift in his intellectual pursuits toward more literary themes. He wrote an essay on Fyodor Dostoyevsky's *The Idiot* and plunged more decisively into the work of translating Baudelaire's *Les fleurs du mal*, a project that he had begun several years before. For his birthday that July, Dora gave him more of what he always wanted: "a number of wonderful books," including an edition of works by Andreas Gryphius, the German baroque playwright and poet who would feature prominently in Benjamin's later study of the *Trauerspiel*, or "mourning play."[30] In October 1917, Benjamin enrolled at the university in Bern; among his courses was a lecture on Baudelaire, along with classes on philosophy and German Romanticism. For the topic of his doctoral dissertation he briefly considered writing on Kant; but by the end of March 1918 he wrote to Scholem that he had settled at last on a topic: the concept of art criticism in German Romanticism.[31]

Throughout these years Scholem and Benjamin remained in nearly unbroken contact. Benjamin wrote his friend as often as possible from Switzerland, and even sent a photo of the newly married couple. Dora was most likely already pregnant when the photo was taken. To his diary Scholem confided: "Walter and Dora's image now always stands before me at my writing desk, and I can converse with them at any time. Dora looks so infinitely beautiful, and Walter truly serious!"[32] In April 1918, Dora gave birth to a son, whom the doting parents named Stefan Rafael (the second name an homage to Dora's recently deceased grandfather).[33] "Among the most wonderful things to see," Benjamin wrote to Scholem, "is what I have observed these past few days: how a father immediately perceives such a small human being as a person, in such a way that the father's own superiority in all matters having to do with existence seems very insignificant in comparison."[34]

In Bern the prospects for suitable housing proved impossible. Only a month after Stefan's birth the family trio was compelled to move to Muri bei Bern, a small village, then having an estimated total of two thousand residents, which lay about four kilometers from the city center. Meanwhile the friendship between Scholem and Benjamin had grown far more profound. Benjamin now wrote "Dear Gerhard," and concluded his letters "Your Walter," though for the time being they still sustained the formality of addressing each other with *Sie* rather than the more

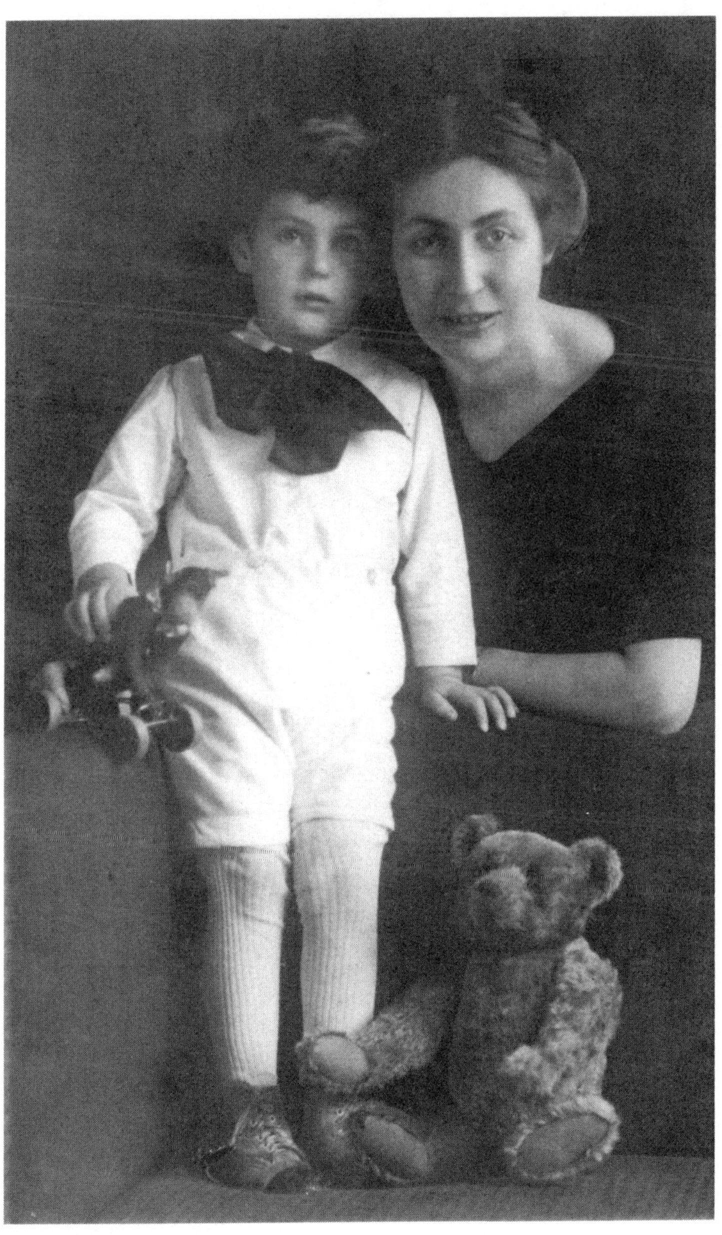

Dora (Kellner) Benjamin with son Stefan, February, 1921

intimate *du*. Shortly after the couple had moved to Muri, Scholem planned an extensive visit, and it was suggested that he take a room nearby. He secured a room in the village that was only a two-minute walk from the Benjamins, and during his stay in Switzerland the bond between the two men gradually deepened. During his visit Scholem first discerned what he called the "basic melancholy" in his friend's temperament, and he also noticed (in his words) "the hysterical elements" in Dora. The couple would often erupt in quarrels. On one occasion when Scholem was invited for dinner he overheard screaming from upstairs, which grew so intense that he felt compelled to leave.[35] The little family remained together officially until their divorce in 1930; but well before that the promise of marital happiness had faded away.

The University of Muri

During his stay in Muri bei Bern Scholem and Benjamin hatched a humorous plan: they would found a fictitious institution of higher learning, which they decided to name "the University of Muri." They drew up academic protocols for the imaginary courses and even drafted a list of library acquisitions. Benjamin was assigned the role of rector, while Scholem was declared "Warden of the School of the Philosophy of Religion."[36] For two young men at the early stages of their academic careers this was far more than a foray into make-believe. Scholem had already embarked on a course of study that would explore the Jewish mystical tradition as a subterranean and anarchic force beneath the respectable edifice of official Judaism. He sought to undermine the authority of nineteenth-century Jewish scholarship (known as the *Wissenschaft des Judentums*) even while he became a virtuoso of its philological methods. Benjamin shared this ambivalence. Although he felt the calling to become a scholar, a vein of rebellion ran through his character that could sometimes sabotage his efforts. For their "fantasy university" Benjamin went so far as to compose satirical book reviews and institutional reports, mocking the rituals that would determine their shared fate in the university system.[37]

This kind of rebellion was not uncommon. Benjamin and Scholem belonged to a generation that was seized by a drive to overturn intellectual authority. Esteemed philosophers of the older generation such as Hermann Cohen were to be read carefully but with suspicion. Cohen's early work, *Kant's Theory of Experience* (first published in 1871), appeared as a monument to be surveyed but then toppled so that its ruins could be sifted for a hidden key. In Muri bei Bern, Benjamin and Scholem passed many hours together reading Cohen's masterpiece but eventually abandoned the task. In "On the Program of the Coming Philosophy," an ambitious essay written in 1918 but unpublished during his lifetime, Benjamin condemned the Kantian and neo-Kantian model of experience as "shallow" and "religiously very infertile."[38] He anticipated a "philosophy of the future" that would revive the religious and metaphysical elements of experience that Kant had banished, even while he continued to feel a strong disliking for Buber's vitalist concept of lived experience, or *Erlebnis.* His dissatisfactions with the rationalist tradition in philosophy may also help to explain why he turned with enthusiasm to the circle of German Romantic philosophers and critics such as Friedrich Schlegel and Novalis.

Romanticism and Criticism

Benjamin wrote his doctoral dissertation swiftly, and by April 1919 he had completed an initial draft. The turn in subject matter, from Kant to Romantic art criticism, was not as abrupt as it may appear. In the introduction, Benjamin notes that the Romantics conceived of *Kritik* in a fashion that paid homage to the Kantian idea of critique: it became "an esoteric term for the incomparable and completed philosophical standpoint." The dissertation fastens almost exclusively on the idea of art criticism, more specifically the criticism of poetry and literature, as it was expounded by Friedrich Schlegel in the *Athenaeum*, the literary journal published by Schlegel and his brother between 1798 and 1800; it also makes use of lectures that Schlegel delivered in Paris and Cologne between 1804 and 1806. Taken as a whole, these sources provide Benjamin with what he considers "the Romantic theory of criticism."[39]

Benjamin argues that the Romantic concept of art criticism draws its major inspiration from Johann Gottlieb Fichte's idea of the "thinking of thinking." Following Fichte's claim that all knowledge begins with the subject's act of self-positing, the Romantics concluded that all knowledge is self-knowledge. In Benjamin's words: "there is in fact no knowledge of an object by a subject. Every instance of knowing is an immanent connection in the absolute." This basic theme of "reflection" informs the Romantic concept of art criticism. "Insofar as criticism is knowledge of the work of art, it is its self-knowledge; insofar as it judges the artwork, this occurs in the latter's self-judgement." The self-reflexive character of art criticism helps to elucidate the true significance of Schlegel's famous remark about Johann Wolfgang von Goethe's novel *Wilhelm Meister's Apprenticeship*: "Fortunately, it is one of those books that judge themselves."[40] From this remark Benjamin derives a general principle that inspired his own practice of criticism: one does not criticize an artwork from a perspective that is exotic to the work itself; on the contrary, criticism is nothing but the artwork's self-realization. This is because the artwork contains "criticizability" as its inner potential. "Every critical understanding of an artistic entity is, as reflection in the entity, nothing other than a higher, self-actively originated degree of this entity's consciousness."[41]

It is perhaps not hard to grasp why Benjamin would have found Schlegel's arguments appealing: they elevate the critic to a position that is nearly equal in authority to the artwork itself.

Criticism is no longer a subjective practice added after the fact to the aesthetic material; it is the objective unfolding of what is already at hand. "The distinctive element in the Romantic concept of criticism," Benjamin explains, "lies in its freedom from any special subjective estimation of the work in a judgement of taste. Valuation is immanent to the objective investigation and knowledge of the work. The critic does not pass judgement on the work; rather, *art itself passes judgement.*" A poet of towering importance such as Goethe might have preferred to dismiss criticism as unnecessary, but Benjamin argues otherwise. He extols the critic as enhancing the merits of the artwork itself. "Not only is criticism, in Romantic art, possible and necessary, but in the theory of Romantic art one cannot avoid the paradox that criticism is valued more highly than works of art."[42]

In June 1919 Benjamin successfully defended his dissertation at the University of Bern before an examining committee that awarded it the highest distinction.[43] Published a year later (and printed by Arthur Scholem, Gerhard's father), the dissertation marked the first major step forward on what Benjamin had every reason to believe would be a promising academic career. But the dissertation was also a statement of personal ambition. In affirming the status of the critic alongside the artwork, Benjamin was also affirming his own importance. Ten years later he would restate his purpose in a letter to Scholem: "The goal I had set for myself has not yet been totally realized, but I am finally getting close. The goal is that I be considered the foremost critic of German literature." The dissertation did not signify a consuming or exclusive interest in the era of German Romanticism, though Benjamin later wrote an important essay on Goethe's *Elective Affinities.* Its true significance lay elsewhere. At a moment when the young scholar was possessed by intellectual ambition, the dissertation gave him an opportunity to explore his own notions of criticism and to begin forging the tools that he would require in his future work. "The problem," he explained, "is that literary criticism is no longer considered a serious genre in Germany and has not been for more than fifty years. If you want to carve out a reputation in the area of criticism, this ultimately means that you must re-create criticism as a genre."[44] In the coming years he would devote himself fully to this task.

4

Angelus Novus

In the years that followed the First World War, Benjamin, together with Dora and Stefan, moved back from Switzerland to Germany. Initially he had hoped that he could stay on at Bern, where the director of his doctoral dissertation, Richard Herbertz, had suggested that he might pursue further work in philosophy and eventually submit the second thesis that was required for his habilitation, or post-doctoral degree. The proposal, however, came to nothing, chiefly due to disagreements between Walter and his parents, who refused to offer the necessary support.[1] For a brief while the little trio stayed with Dora's parents in Vienna, but they soon returned to Berlin, where, in March 1920, they moved into the Benjamin family residence on Delbrückstrasse. "My parents," Benjamin explained to Scholem, "have ordered us categorically to live at home with them, since my father's bad financial situation no longer allows him to support us away from home."[2]

In Germany the political atmosphere was volatile. The new republic, founded at Weimar after the Kaiser's abdication, was born from the humiliating experience of military defeat, and it was burdened with reparations that left the country in economic disarray. Conditions in the Benjamin home, too, were riven with conflict. Emil's firm was no longer thriving, and there was a palpable tension between father and son. After little more than two months the young family felt compelled to move out. Benjamin described it as a "total split." What had once been a stream of melancholy in his character now became a flood. "Things have almost never been as miserable for me not in my entire life." To Scholem he offered little explanation, noting only that he had "plunged very deeply." It was necessary "to avoid the memory of it if I am able ever to surface again."[3]

Romantic Anti-Capitalism

His future was now more uncertain than ever before, and the prospect of becoming a professor seemed remote. He briefly entertained thoughts of becoming a bookseller or perhaps a publisher, but his father denied him the necessary capital for launching the venture. Dora's parents, however, despite "extreme sacrifices," were willing to offer their conditional support.[4] All the same, Benjamin did not feel that he could wholly abandon his plans for an academic career. In the summer of 1921 he made the journey back to Heidelberg, where he encountered philosophers such as Karl Jaspers and his old teacher Heinrich Rickert. He also participated in sociological "evening discussions" organized by Marianne Weber, the widow of the recently deceased Max Weber.

The Heidelberg circle around Max and Marianne Weber convened some of the most original thinkers of the era, including the Hegelian-Marxist philosopher Georg Lukács and the heterodox Marxist philosopher Ernst Bloch. The circle seems to have inspired Benjamin to write an exploratory sketch, "Capitalism as Religion," in which he took some tentative steps toward a style of social criticism that in previous years had seldom aroused his interest. The immediate inspiration was the "Weber-thesis," namely, the socio-historical hypothesis that early-modern capitalists had found in Calvinist teaching an "ethic" that furnished them with a spiritual justification for this-worldly conduct. Weber had formulated this thesis only as an attempt at sociological understanding; Benjamin twisted the thesis around into an anti-capitalist critique. Capitalism, he explained, does not simply draw upon religious doctrine as a spiritual support; rather, capitalism is *itself* a religion. But it is an odd kind of religion: it is oriented not toward progress but rather worldly catastrophe. "Capitalism is entirely without precedent," Benjamin explained. "It is a religion which offers not the reform of existence but its complete destruction."

Benjamin's critique of capitalism as a religion is neither Weberian nor really Marxist: it best aligns with a sensibility that Georg Lukács had once called "romantic anti-capitalism."[5] As early as 1907 Lukács had been reading German Romantics such as Schlegel, Friedrich Schelling, and Novalis, and he found in their works the sources for a protest against modern disenchantment. Later works such as *The Theory of the Novel* (1916) expressed an aesthetic longing for a past era or non-bourgeois future "whose paths were illuminated by the light of the stars."[6] As Lukács moved toward Marxism, the romantic critique of capitalism receded and gave way to a far more rational style of analysis that assigned the working class a pivotal role in human history. But the youthful complaint against the loss of cultural meaning did not wholly vanish: the diagnosis of *reification* in his masterful synthesis of Hegelian and Marxist philosophy, *History and Class Consciousness* (1923), borrows from Weber its basic image of modern society as an iron cage from which the spirit has fled.

In the years immediately following the First World War,

the sensibility of romantic anti-capitalism became a commonplace among intellectuals on the left. One can detect a similar posture not only in Lukács and Bloch but also in key figures who participated in the short-lived Bavarian socialist republic, such as Ernst Toller and Gustav Landauer.[7] The term may also apply to Benjamin as well. In 1919 he had just read Ernst Bloch's *The Spirit of Utopia* (first published in 1918; revised in 1923), a work that expressed both despair for "expired civilizations" and hope for "the one salvation."[8] Fusing political radicalism with religious eschatology, Bloch wrote that "the human soul embraces everything, including the other side which is *not yet.* Hope alone is what we want," and we look for its signs "scattered into every part of the world, hidden in the darkness of the lived moment, promised in the shape of the absolute question."[9] In elaborating his unusual ideas Bloch braided together Marxism and Christianity. But the actual answer to his question remained inchoate. In the concluding lines to the book he wrote of "the will to the Kingdom" in which all tributaries would converge, "the Soul, the Messiah, and the Apocalypse."[10]

Benjamin had first befriended Bloch during the war while they were both living abroad, and he praised Bloch as "the only person of consequence I have gotten to know in Switzerland thus far." Their conversations proved tremendously stimulating, if only because Bloch "so often challenged my rejection of *every* political trend."[11] To his friend Ernst Schoen, Benjamin admitted in confidence that Bloch's book "exhibits enormous deficiencies," but he hastened to note that "I am indebted to the book for much that is substantive." It was "the only book on which, as a truly contemporaneous and contemporary utterance, I can take my own measure," since "the author stands alone and philosophically stands up for his cause, while almost everything we read today of a philosophical nature written by our contemporaries is derivative and adulterated. You can never get a handle on its moral center and, at the most, it leads you to the origin of the evil that it itself represents."[12]

Despite feeling some ambivalence about Bloch's ideas, in the early 1920s Benjamin himself was inclined toward many themes associated with romantic anti-capitalism. Despair over existing political reality intermingled with a radical hope for a not yet realized utopia, the vague outlines of which were prefigured in past traditions, both Marxist and religious. One of the best testaments to this sensibility is the unnamed sketch that Benjamin's literary executors later titled the "Theological-Political Fragment." In this enigmatic document, Benjamin seems to deny that messianic themes have any application whatsoever to secular political history. But his denial does not entail an outright *rejection* of the messianic; on the contrary, by drawing a stark separation between the "secular order" and the "Divine Kingdom," he wishes to protect them from mutual contamination. The name for such a contamination would be "theocracy." Benjamin thus concludes that the messianic in the genuine sense would represent not the culmination or "telos" of history but its "terminus."

> Only the Messiah himself completes all history, in the sense that he alone redeems, completes, creates its relation to the messianic. For this reason nothing that is historical can relate itself, from its own ground, to anything messianic. . . . Therefore, the secular order cannot be built on the idea of the Divine Kingdom, and theocracy has no political but only a religious meaning.[13]

Much like his remarks on capitalism as a religion, the theological-political fragment suggests that Benjamin wishes to *isolate* religion from political reality, since he fears that any dreams of their fusion would produce only monsters. The hidden target of this argument remains uncertain. But it would not be implausible to read it as a warning against the explosive consequences of uniting religion with politics in an extremist version of Zionism. We should not forget that Scholem himself was consumed with a similar anxiety. This hostility to the fusion of theological and political themes may explain why Benjamin lavishes such praise on Bloch. "To have repudiated with utmost vehemence the political significance of theocracy," Benjamin writes, "is the cardinal merit of Bloch's *Spirit of Utopia.*"[14]

To be sure, the ambiguities of the text may reflect the fact that its author was experimenting with problems for which he had not yet found a clear solution. Even the dating of the text remains ambiguous. Some believe it was written in the later 1930s; others, including Scholem, find it more plausible that Benjamin wrote it between 1920 and 1921. The reference to Bloch's *Spirit of Utopia* (published in its first edition in 1918) would seem to suggest that Scholem was correct. But a puzzling fact remains. In one of his last and most celebrated essays, often called the "Theses" on the philosophy of history, Benjamin would return to the idea of the "messianic" as a force outside the historical continuum. Much of the thematic material that is developed later in the "Theses" also appears in the theological-political fragment, so it may be tempting to conclude that they were written in close succession. Surprisingly, however, the two texts come to opposite conclusions. In the "Theses," Benjamin *welcomes* the intrusion of the messianic into history; the theological idea of a messianic or discontinuous time furnishes the redemptive principle without which there can be no prospect for genuine revolution. In the earlier theological-political fragment, however, Benjamin *repudiates* any such intrusion; he warns that the messianic has its own integrity but has no valid application to the political world.

In other writings from the period immediately following the war, Benjamin gradually came to feel that it might be necessary to breach the wall of separation between theology and politics. One can glimpse the change especially in his "Critique of Violence," an essay written in 1921 and published that same year in the *Archiv für Sozialwissenschaft und Sozialpolitik* (the journal co-edited by Weber and others in the Heidelberg circle). Benjamin develops his argument with reference to Georges Sorel's *Réflexions sur la violence* (originally 1908), in which the French anarcho-syndicalist sought to understand the role of myths as motivational frameworks for working-class conduct. A general strike, Sorel argues, can furnish the proletariat what it most needs: a "catastrophic myth" that will inspire violence and revolution.[15] Benjamin, though partly inspired by Sorel, rejects any celebration of mythic violence and draws a sharp distinction between mythic violence and divine violence. "Just as in all spheres God opposes myth, mythic violence is confronted by the divine." For Benjamin this divide cannot be bridged. "If mythic violence is lawmaking, divine violence is law-destroying; if the former sets boundaries, the latter boundlessly destroys them; if mythic violence brings at once guilt and retribution, divine power only expiates; . . . if the former is bloody, the latter is lethal without spilling blood."[16]

The argument is provocative, but the explanations are unclear. How could power be lethal without spilling blood? Is the destruction of law always advantageous? Is the intrusion of the "divine" always to be welcomed? Benjamin explores these questions but provides few answers. Historical context may assist us in understanding what he had in mind. The distinction between mythic and divine violence may refer, however obliquely, to the state's brutal suppression of the Bavarian Republic. Benjamin means to criticize the bourgeois state that deploys "mythic violence" to preserve the current legal and political order against the challenges of revolution. Divine power, by contrast, is "lethal" only in the sense that it puts an end to conventional law. "Mythic violence is bloody power over mere life for its own sake," he explains. "Divine violence is pure power over all life for the sake of the living."[17]

Around this time ruminations on the "divine" appear with

some frequency in Benjamin's writing. This may help to explain why he felt so captivated by *Angelus Novus*, a small aquarelle of an angel by Paul Klee. Painted circa 1920, it was first exhibited in May and June of that year at a gallery in Munich. Many scholars have pondered the question of why Benjamin found the image so arresting: it portrays a fabulous creature, human in both face and stature but with birdlike talons and arms raised like wings. Its eyes are turned to the right, as if transfixed in either fear or fascination, by something just beyond the frame. Benjamin saw the painting in Munich and purchased it for one thousand marks, but asked Scholem if he might keep it safe for him until his housing situation was resolved. By late November 1921 the angel finally arrived in Berlin, where it hung on the wall of Benjamin's room in Delbrückstrasse. Iconic and enigmatic, the painting became for Benjamin a kind of muse, and it would continue to inspire his thinking to the very end of his life, most memorably in his "Theses" on the philosophy of history.[18]

Klee's painting also inspired an editorial venture. In August 1921 the Heidelberg publisher Richard Weissbach, well known for his work in promoting literary expressionism, offered to support Benjamin's plan to found a new journal that would be called, like the painting, *Angelus Novus*.[19] Benjamin wrote to Scholem with great enthusiasm about his proposal, and he even drafted an editorial announcement for the first issue in which he boldly declared his intentions. The statement is illuminating not least because it echoes themes he had expressed in his dissertation on the concept of criticism. "The function of great criticism," he writes, "is not, as is often thought, to instruct by means of historical descriptions or to educate through comparisons." The purpose of criticism is "to cognize by immersing itself in the object." Resisting the superficial allure of historicization, the critic's task would be "to account for the truth of works, a task just as essential for literature as for philosophy." Benjamin declares that he would have little tolerance for either "spiritualist occultism" or "political obscurantism." Instead the journal would place its highest value on "rationalism" and "philosophical universality." The editorial statement concludes with the admission that if a journal would strive for contemporary relevance it must resign itself to an "ephemeral existence [*das Ephemere*]."[20] Benjamin illustrated this point with a Talmudic legend: "the angels—who are created anew every moment in countless droves—are brought into being so that, after they have sung their hymns before God, then cease and vanish away into nothingness."[21]

Benjamin launched eagerly into planning the details for the journal's first issue, and he even wrote up a list to name those who would be responsible for its various topics. Among those he wished to secure for the project were: Scholem for Jewish themes, Bloch for philosophy, the Hebrew writer S. Y. Agnon for literature, Florens Christian Rang (a former government minister and theologian who befriended Benjamin at the time) for politics, and Ferdinand Cohrs (an evangelical pastor who was once in the Berlin Free Students' Union with Benjamin) for theology.[22] For the first issue Benjamin was also keen to publish poems by his late friend Heinle. To Scholem he made it clear that the journal would not be "specifically Jewish," a fact that may have deterred Scholem from contributing much energy to the project.[23]

Despite Benjamin's best efforts, however, the plans for the proposed journal eventually came to naught. Financial considerations forced Weissbach to suspend, at least temporarily, all arrangements for publishing the journal. In a Rosh Hashanah letter dated October 1, 1922, and addressed to both Scholem and his fiancée Escha Burchardt, Benjamin confided the sad news with playful indirection: "the Angelus announced his own departure just as yesterday came to an end, as if he wanted to prove one last time what a good Jew he is. He has moved into his old house in the clay-colored sky and the editor's throne of honor in my heart is empty." His disappointment was mixed, however, with the sense that the reversal of plans had restored "my old freedom of choice." Like the angels in the Talmudic legend, his plans for the journal proved evanescent.[24]

Although hopes for the journal did not come to fruition, the angel in Klee's painting became a figure of such enduring significance for Benjamin that in his correspondence he endowed it with an independent life. Occasionally he even indulged himself with imaginary reports on its activities. Charlotte Wolff, a psychologist who befriended both Dora and Walter, later recalled her impressions of Benjamin in the early twenties:

> I see Walter Benjamin sitting behind a large table piled high with books and with his manuscripts, the walls of his room lined with books from floor to ceiling except for one small space where there hung a painting by Paul Klee, 'The Angel.' [*sic*] To him the picture was a living being, and he referred to it as if it were a person. The geometrical thin-lined design escaped the grasp of my imagination, but I accepted his valuation of it without question.[25]

Despite the collapse of his plans for the new journal, Benjamin could take some comfort in the fact that he had just completed his sustained critical essay on Goethe's novel *Elective Affinities*, and he read it aloud to Wolff during one of her visits.[26] He also sent off a copy of the essay to Scholem, chastising him in advance should there be any delay in sending back comments, and boasting that "here great and small alike claim to be waiting for it."[27] Initially Benjamin had hoped that the essay might appear in his own journal, but its actual publication would be delayed by nearly two years. Eventually, it was published in 1924 in the *Neue deutsche Beiträge*, the short-lived journal founded and edited by the esteemed Viennese essayist and librettist Hugo von Hofmannsthal.[28]

Hope for the Hopeless

Perhaps more than any other early work, the essay on *Elective Affinities* gave Benjamin an extraordinary chance to display his skills as a critic of literature. The topic was well suited for this purpose. It would not be an exaggeration to say that Goethe occupies a seat in the German literary canon much like Shakespeare's in the English-speaking world. Venturing into a debate over Goethe with more established scholars was a high-stakes game for which Benjamin had much to lose but also much to gain, and he pursued the task without restraint. Completed in 1922, the essay was nothing less than a frontal assault on the self-appointed guardians of contemporary taste. Its selected target was Friedrich Gundolf, the author of the formidable biographical study *Goethe* (a work more than eight hundred pages in length, first published in 1916). Gundolf (born Gundelfinger) was a German Jew by origin who had risen to the heights of the German academic establishment. In 1916 he had secured a prestigious professorship at Heidelberg, where he taught from 1916 onward; but he was also a key figure in the George Kreis, the esoteric literary circle that had grown up in cultlike reverence around the symbolist poet Stefan George. When Benjamin passed through Heidelberg in 1921 he had the opportunity to hear Gundolf speak, and he noted that in person the professor appeared "terribly feeble and harmless," an impression that was quite different from how he came across in his written work. In composing his essay on Goethe's novel Benjamin had set himself a polemical task: "the legally binding condemnation and execution of Friedrich Gundolf."[29]

But the essay also had a more intellectual purpose. As stated in its opening lines, Benjamin wished to demonstrate his own conception of "critique," which he distinguished sharply from "commentary." These two modes of literary study appeared to be separated by a chasm that was not only methodological but also metaphysical. "Critique," Benjamin explained, "seeks the truth content of a work of art," while "commentary" explores its "material content." To underscore the distinction Benjamin proposed a curious analogy. A literary work is like a burning funeral pyre. The commentator looks upon it like a chemist who is interested only in the "wood and ash" that remain after the fire is extinguished, whereas the critic stands before the pyre like an alchemist who sees in the flame the enigmatic remnants of what is still alive. For Benjamin, however, Gundolf's study of Goethe was neither critique nor commentary, and it embodied everything that he found distasteful in the then dominant methods of literary study. It reflected little more than the "thoughtless dogma" that a human life could be likened to a work of art. With this premise Gundolf had elevated the person of Goethe into a "hero-as-creator" whose life became an aestheticized object of "blasphemous profundity." The biography thereby lost all connection with truth; instead it devolved into a myth, and served as an "ungainly pedestal" upon which its hero could become an object of veneration for the George circle and its "esoteric doctrine." Benjamin's polemic was unrestrained. When reading Gundolf's book one felt as if one were in "a jungle where words swing themselves, like chattering monkeys, from branch to branch, from bombast to bombast."[30]

Such withering assault on one of the most esteemed literary scholars of the time was no doubt audacious, but it seems that Benjamin meant every word in deadly earnest. He was convinced that the practice of literary criticism had fallen into disuse and that it was his mission to infuse it with new life. "For critique ultimately shows in the work of art the virtual possibility of formulating the work's truth content as the highest philosophical problem."[31] Goethe's novel thereby became a staging ground for his own critical debut.

The choice of this particular novel was hardly incidental. Written in 1809, *Elective Affinities* is often ranked among the author's greatest but most perplexing achievements, and Benjamin wished to display his acumen by exercising all of his interpretive powers upon a work that does not easily yield its secrets. On its surface, it consists in a familiar story of romance gone awry. Set on a country estate, the novel tells the tale of Eduard and Charlotte, a married couple who welcome into their lives two individuals, Captain Otto and Ottilie (who happens to be Charlotte's niece). There follows a complex of illicit affairs: the Captain falls in love with Charlotte, and Eduard falls in love with Ottilie. This crossing is said to demonstrate a scientific principle of chemical bonding, or "elective affinities" (*die Wahlverwandtschaften*) from which the novel gets its name. Such affinities, however, prove far less stable in personal affairs than in chemistry. The Captain and Charlotte share little more than a forbidden kiss, while the affair between Eduard and Ottilie yields a child. But Charlotte also bears a child, whose resemblance to the Captain symbolizes the fact of their illicit love. Ottilie, however, is young and emotionally volatile; in a fit of jealousy, she drowns the child and soon afterward starves herself to death. Eduard then dies from illness. Charlotte and the Captain live out their lives together, and they decide to bury Eduard and Ottilie side by side, so that they might at least be united in death.

This tangled and tragic narrative is rich in meanings that could arouse the interest of any serious critic. But it may have also appealed to Benjamin for a further, more personal reason. By 1921 his own marriage to Dora was coming apart at the seams. Dora had fallen in love with Ernst Schoen (Walter's former schoolmate, and later an important figure in Weimar-era broadcasting). Then Walter promptly fell in love with Jula Cohn (the sister of Alfred Cohn, who was also a friend from Walter's schooldays). During his 1921 stay in Heidelberg, Walter also saw Jula, who as it happens belonged to the group surrounding Gundolf. By the time Benjamin finally published his essay on *Elective Affinities*, his marriage with Dora had wholly collapsed, though they remained on relatively amicable terms and stayed together in the short term chiefly for Stefan's sake. Although the divorce was not made official until 1930, the separation was public knowledge. The title page of Benjamin's Goethe essay announces, without embarrassment, that it is "dedicated to Jula Cohn." Benjamin was clearly aware of the manifold echoes between literature and life, and he took personal pride in the essay as one of his greatest achievements. So he could not resist adding a secret allusion to himself. In the midst of the essay, he abruptly adds a comment about the goddess Aphrodite, who is born from the water. Her beauty, he explains, is therefore "praised at flowing rivers and fountains," after which he notes that "one of the Oceanides is named *Schönfliess* [or, "beautiful flow"]."[32] Schönflies, of course, is the family name of Walter's mother Pauline, and it is also one of his own middle names.

Why this secret allusion to the maternal family name? Several reasons suggest themselves. For Benjamin the story of Ottilie's drowning of the newborn child, followed by her own apparent suicide by starvation, may have struck a highly personal chord, since it recalled the suicide of his friend Fritz Heinle only a few years before. Whatever the biographical considerations, however, Benjamin wished most of all to fasten his critical attention on the novel itself. Leaving aside the historicist and biographical matters that had preoccupied Gundolf, Benjamin meant to disclose the work's "truth content as the highest philosophical problem." The enigmatic figure of Ottilie appears at the novel's center. Taciturn and ghostly, she is "a semblance of living beauty." Like Aphrodite, water is her element. Like water, Ottilie appears as a *beautiful semblance* whose secret cannot be conjured away. "Thus, in the face of everything beautiful, the idea of unveiling becomes that of the impossibility of unveiling. It is the idea of art criticism. The task of art criticism is not to lift the veil but rather, through the most precise knowledge of it as a veil, to raise itself for the first time to the true view of the beautiful."[33]

The most precise knowledge of it as a veil. For Benjamin the figure of Ottilie is not an enigma to be resolved; it is nothing less than the enigma of art itself. How else can we understand water as the ambivalent simile that governs the entire novel? Water, Benjamin explains, has a "strange magic." For "on the one hand, it is black, dark, unfathomable; but on the other hand, it is reflecting, clear, and clarifying." Water is therefore an ambivalent symbol: it signifies death but also hope. Benjamin concludes his essay with a meditation on hope, which makes a symbolic appearance in the novel like a "falling star" that passes over the lovers' heads. *Elpis*, the Greek word for hope, remains (in his words) "the last of the primal words." It expresses not only the blessing that the survivors in the novel must believe in; it also expresses "the hope of redemption that we nourish for all the dead." As some critics have observed, this notion of redemptive hope appears to draw inspiration not from Judaism but from the Christian idea of *apokatastasis*, which Benjamin had encountered chiefly through his readings of Gottfried Leibniz.[34]

Plays of Mourning

Even while Benjamin was still writing the Goethe essay, he continued to seek academic support for his habilitation. When the faculty at Bern proved unreceptive, he turned first to Heidelberg, but found prospects there just as unlikely. As he explained in a letter to Scholem in December 1922, "a Jew by name of [Karl] Mannheim will apparently do his habilitation there with Alfred Weber." Mannheim, a young sociologist, had the further advantage that he was connected with Bloch and Lukács, and was therefore a familiar presence in the circle around Marianne Weber. The reference to Mannheim's Jewish heritage was presumably an acknowledgment of ongoing prejudice. As Max Weber had observed in 1917, academic life is a "mad hazard," and for a young scholar seeking a habilitation he found it difficult to offer any encouragement. "If he is a Jew," he added, "of course you can only say, *lasciate ogni Speranza*," or, *abandon all hope*.[35] To be sure, the founding of the Weimar Republic had brought a newly democratic spirit into academic life: in 1926 Mannheim himself succeeded in securing himself an academic degree. But Benjamin continued to feel the sting of rejection. His failures in Bern and Heidelberg left him in a state of serious depression, and his dark mood was only aggravated by quarrels with his parents, whose "pronounced pettiness and need for control" had turned into "a torture devouring all the energy I have to work and all my joy in life."[36]

He then turned to the University of Frankfurt, where he believed that family ties to his great-uncle Arthur Schönflies and others might enhance his chances.[37] During a visit there in the winter of 1922–1923, he also had the opportunity to visit with Franz Rosenzweig, the Jewish philosopher whose book *Der Stern der Erlösung* ("The Star of Redemption," 1921) had left a strong impression on him and would influence his theory of tragedy.[38] He also briefly entertained the thought of starting a bookstore, but he devoted most of his efforts to the campaign for writing a habilitation.

The proposed topic of the habilitation was the *Trauerspiel* (or "mourning play"), a genre of baroque theater that had emerged in German-speaking lands during the mid-seventeenth century. This was an unusual dramatic form that most previous scholars had largely neglected and even disparaged, but to Benjamin its marginal, even esoteric character made it all the more intriguing. His interest was first aroused as early as 1916, when he sketched two short commentaries on the difference between *Trauerspiel* and tragedy.[39] The distinction, he explained, hinges on different conceptions of historical time. Tragedy seeks to represent historical greatness, but historical time is "infinite in every direction" and cannot reach fulfillment. The idea of genuinely fulfilled time appears only in the Bible where it manifests itself as "messianic time." The tragic hero does not live in a biblical cosmos; he lives purely as an individual and dies "because no one can live in fulfilled time." The *Trauerspiel*, however, does not conform to the genre of conventional tragedy. It is a "hybrid genre" that portrays all human action within "the restricted space of earthly existence." Human conduct in a *Trauerspiel* is locked into a game of mere repetition where all events remain "allegorical schemata" that can never reach fulfillment.[40]

The *Trauerspiel* was a dramatic form that reflected the religious anxiety and violence of post-Reformation Germany, when princes were waging war over both theology and territory. Among its authors were exemplars of the mid-seventeenth-century baroque such as Andreas Gryphius and Daniel Casper von Lohenstein, literary masters from the so-called "Second Silesian School" whose plays frequently involved court intrigue, speechifying, ghostly apparitions, and spectacular displays of bloodshed. Benjamin's attraction to this rather exotic body of work may seem surprising, especially if we consider his stated ambition to distinguish himself as the foremost critic of his day. It is helpful to note, however, that in its overwrought style the *Trauerspiel* of the seventeenth century bears some resemblance to the expressionist movement of the early twentieth century. In his study Benjamin remarks on the "striking analogies" that connect modern German literature to the baroque era. The analogy becomes apparent chiefly in the "vigorous style of language" and the "violence of manner" that are shared in common by what he calls "ages of decline" (*Zeiten des Verfalls*).[41] For neither the expressionist era nor the baroque can be praised as ages of "authentic artistic practice." Both are epochs in which aesthetic style is used "to conceal the deficiencies of valid products in literature."[42] No doubt there were ample grounds for discerning such an analogy. Not unlike the baroque era, the early phase of the Weimar Republic was a time of great violence and political disarray. Military defeat, a flu epidemic, socialist uprisings, and the Kapp putsch were followed by the occupation of the Ruhr and the hyperinflation of 1923. Benjamin's critical study of the *Trauerspiel* was therefore, covertly, a study of his own time.

But there is a further reason that may help to explain Benjamin's fascination with the plays of the German baroque. Following the successful completion of his dissertation he was nourishing an even stronger interest in problems of theology. The religious themes that had already been apparent in works such as the "Theological-Political Fragment," the "Critique of Violence," and the sketch on "Capitalism as Religion" now converged in a mature study in which Benjamin turned his full attention to theological and political themes that had preoccupied European philosophers during the Reformation and Counter-Reformation. To explore these themes with precision, however, required philosophical guidance. Among the sources he consulted for his study were writings by the legal and political scholar Carl Schmitt, especially his *Political Theology* (first published in 1922).

Schmitt, a conservative Catholic, was especially alert to seeming weaknesses in liberal theories of sovereignty. In a bold dictum that would become famous among denizens of his political theology, Schmitt declared that "All significant concepts of the modern theory of the state are *secularized theological concepts.*"[43] With this insight he meant to suggest not only a historical lineage; he meant to imply that all liberal theories of sovereignty suffered from a near-fatal weakness. According to Schmitt, modern political liberalism had developed a concept of the constitutional state that was consistent with its vision of a disenchanted nature. Most of all, liberalism reflected the rationalist metaphysics of the eighteenth century. Just as deism had sought to banish the miracle from the world, so too the constitutional state appeared as if it were a mechanistic order of positive law, in which the miracle of personal decision was minimized if not eliminated entirely.[44] The liberal idea of the state was therefore left with an irresolvable problem: especially in moments of crisis the system of law alone could not decide upon the proper course of action. In such moments, constitutional liberalism came face to face with its own theoretical limits: it confronted the deficiencies in any theory of state power that presupposes the secular notion of a world without miracles. Schmitt did not mean to imply that theology itself was truly necessary for politics. He meant that all politics, even secular politics, must rely on a *quasi*-theological moment of absolute decision that law alone cannot explain. As a matter of principle, he claimed, this decision cannot be altogether banished from the legal order. To drive home this thought his book opens with a lapidary phrase: "Sovereign is he who decides upon the exception."[45]

To be sure, Schmitt's concept of sovereignty was not the only theoretical resource that inspired Benjamin as he began to compose his study of the *Trauerspiel*. But it was significant enough that in 1930, when the book was finally published, he sent Schmitt a copy with a letter of gratitude, writing that "you will immediately note how much the book owes to you in its presentation of the theory of sovereignty in the seventeenth century." He added that Schmitt's study of dictatorship had provided him with some confirmation of his own thoughts for how to research the philosophy of art.[46] Many years later, Schmitt would refer at length to Benjamin's book in his work *Hamlet or Hecuba* (published in 1956).[47] Notwithstanding the open acknowledgment of its debt to Schmitt, however, Benjamin's study of the *Trauerspiel* should not be read as a mere repetition of Schmitt's political-theological arguments. On the contrary; it borrows some of its essential claims from Schmitt only to subject those claims to a critical dismantling.

The key to Benjamin's study is that the figures of royal power who populate the stage in the *Trauerspiel* are not exemplars of sovereign decision. Unlike the muscular authorities in Schmitt's political theology, the personalities in the *Trauerspiel* have little power to change their fate. They are condemned to a "bare creaturely condition" that has been stripped of redemptive meaning and enjoys no access to the divine. The kings and queens lack worldly power. Like the royalty on playing cards, they are mere images of authority or puppets in a dumb show: their actions have sound and fury but signify nothing. Looming over all of these characters is the pervasive temperament of melancholia that was immortalized in the famous sixteenth-century engraving by Albrecht Dürer. The world to which the characters are condemned offers little promise: although it is apparently a historical world, it portrays history as fallen nature or a field of ruins. A common feature of the *Trauerspiel* is "to heap up fragments uninterruptedly, without any well-defined idea of a goal." The lonely figure who surveys this ruinous landscape is the prince, "the paradigm of the melancholic" whose introspection and indecision bear witness to the "frailty" of all humanity. Among the more startling conclusions of the book is that the pensive prince in Shakespeare's *Hamlet* is best understood not as the hero of a genuine tragedy. Rather, he is the final specimen of the *Trauerspiel* at the moment of its decline.[48]

The implicit lesson of Benjamin's study is that the baroque sovereign possesses neither the power nor the decisiveness that would be required for effective political action. The sovereign is an allegory; he embodies *weakness rather than strength*. With this conclusion, however, Benjamin calls into question the key premise of political theology. Implicitly, it seems, he has revealed a major deficiency in Schmitt's arguments. For how could a sovereign who is paralyzed by indecision serve as an analogue to God? To this question Benjamin does not offer a promising political alternative. Instead he turns away from politics altogether.

For if there can be no true analogy between political and divine authority, then it would seem that humanity is condemned to a wholly directionless wandering among the ruins of history. Life itself appears as a *Trauerspiel*, an allegory of mere transience, and history appears as "the realm of dead things, the presumed infinity of empty hopes."[49] A more melancholy lesson could hardly be imagined. Surprisingly, however, Benjamin does not rest content with this conclusion. In the final pages of his study, he introduces a Christian motif that brings about a startling "reversal" (*Umschwung*) in his analysis.[50] The "melancholy immersion" of the human being in a debased world is not a permanent condition. Rather, all earthly things are allegories of mere transience that gain their ultimate meaning only through the grace that is granted by a world-transcendent God. "For it is precisely in visions of the intoxication of destruction, visions in which everything earthly turns to a field of rubble, that there is revealed not so much the ideal of allegorical immersion as its limit."[51] With this reversal the allegorist awakens from the nightmare of mortality to the possibility of *resurrection*. All that is transient must pass away; all allegories of transience, even human bones, are therefore signs that point not to death but to "holy salvation."[52]

The *Trauerspiel* study is brilliant, but also notoriously difficult to read, and at the time some considered it nearly indecipherable. In May 1923, Benjamin visited Frankfurt in the hopes that he might secure the support of faculty there for his habilitation; but Hans Cornelius, a professor of philosophy, refused to act as sponsor.[53] Franz Schultz, a literary scholar who was then serving as dean, responded somewhat more favorably, not least because it had been partly his idea that Benjamin should write on the topic of "German Baroque Literature."[54] Benjamin completed most of the study in the spring of 1924 on Capri, where he engaged in long conversations with other visitors to the island such as Ernst Bloch, and also with a new, intriguing acquaintance, a Latvian woman named Asja Lacis.[55] By the time

Benjamin returned to Germany in the fall the full manuscript was nearly finished. He wrote the last portions in Berlin in December and then sent them off by mail to Schultz. Benjamin feared that his chances were slim. To Scholem he wrote that he did not intend to submit the full text of the introduction, since it was a piece of "unmitigated chutzpah." It consisted in "neither more nor less than the prolegomena to epistemology." All the same, he wrote, he was pleased to have written it. He seemed especially delighted at the thought that his new epigraph, a quotation from Goethe's theory of color, "will make people's jaws drop."[56]

Some months would pass, however, before Benjamin heard anything from the faculty in Frankfurt. Schultz apparently felt that the work would damage his own reputation and therefore withdrew his support.[57] Eventually the study was passed along to Hans Cornelius to be considered for a habilitation in aesthetics; it was officially submitted in mid-May 1925. Cornelius, however, found it "extremely difficult to read," and further reported that "I was unable—despite repeated, concentrated efforts—to derive a comprehensible meaning from [this work]." He therefore refused to recommend the author's work for habilitation in art history. As he explained, "I am unable to ignore my misgiving that the author, with his incomprehensible mode of expression—which must be interpreted as signifying a lack of scholarly clarity—cannot serve as a guide for students in this area."[58] In mid-July the faculty of philosophy issued its decision: it officially moved to reject Benjamin's candidacy. To spare him the humiliation of outright rejection, however, it was suggested that Benjamin be advised to withdraw the manuscript himself. Schultz, in his role as dean, was charged with the task of informing the candidate of the unhappy news.

Among scholars it is now a widespread opinion that the university's verdict was an unforgivable error. Howard Eiland and Michael Jennings write, "With the rejection of Benjamin's submission, the philosophic faculty of the University of Frankfurt brought down on itself a scandal that continues to cast its shadow today."[59] Benjamin himself saw it as a miscarriage of justice and at first responded in anger. To Scholem (who had recently moved to Palestine) he wrote that he felt that Schultz had acted "in extremely bad faith," since he was the one who had opposed a candidacy in literary history and sent the thesis to the philosophy faculty. But Benjamin then declared himself ready to turn the page. "All in all," he wrote, "I am glad. The Old Franconian stage route following the stations of the local university is not my way." As if still immersed in the image world of the *Trauerspiel*, he described Frankfurt as "the most bitter wasteland." His hopes for an academic career now lay in ruins. He nevertheless planned to move ahead with publication of the manuscript, thanks in part to a favorable recommendation from Hofmannsthal, who saw in sections of the manuscript signs of "absolute mastery."[60]

Notwithstanding the striking originality of his work, Benjamin was perhaps right to say that a university career was not the most suitable path. Academic institutions, after all, typically hug the shores of convention, and if he had secured a professorship, he would likely have found himself tethered to standards that would have only inhibited his freedom of imagination. Along with this newfound freedom, however, there came the obvious risks—of penury and rejection, alongside the intellectual aimlessness that may arise if one resists swimming with the tide. In the coming years he would confront both the uncertainty and the promise of his new life as a critic without a home. To Scholem he wrote that his immediate plan was to embark on "a long trip," to travel by freighter from Hamburg to Italy and Spain. It was his "burning desire to bask again this summer in the glow of the August and September sun that shines upon the southernmost tip of Europe."[61]

5

The Wanderer

In the late summer of 1925, Benjamin boarded the *Cantania*, a freighter that took him away from Hamburg and out into the Atlantic. It then sailed southward past the western coast of Spain, through the Straits of Gibraltar, then northward past both Alicante and Barcelona and on toward Naples. In a letter to Jula Cohn, he described "a singular aria of the most comfortable living conditions: in every foreign city you are given your room, indeed a small, somehow vagabond-like household, and you don't have to bother at all with hotels, rooms and guests. At the moment I'm on deck, before me lies Genoa in the evening, and all around me the sound of tradeships laden with goods like the updated 'music of the world.' "[1] He finally disembarked in Naples, where he joined two acquaintances from Frankfurt, Siegfried Kracauer and Theodor Wiesengrund Adorno, with whom he would travel on to Capri.

Mediterranean Interlude

The precarity of his new situation was clear. Benjamin was hardly a true vagabond, but he knew that to realize his intellectual ambitions of becoming a critic he would need to do without the comforts of an academic post. Exiled from the German university system, he turned his attention with renewed passion to modern French literature. Much like his ex-wife Dora, he knew that work as a translator might at least supplement his income. As early as 1914 he had been translating Baudelaire's *Tableaux parisiens*, and even while completing his study of the *Trauerspiel* he continued to translate other portions of the *Fleurs du mal.* In 1923 he published the translations of Baudelaire in a German edition to which he added a prefatory essay, "The Task of the Translator." The translation essay, though brief, is rich with insight into the "bottomless depths of language." All translations, Benjamin claims, mark a stage in the "eternal life" of a work; they pay homage to the "suprahistorical kinship" that connects all languages to one another." Through translation, languages continue to grow "until the messianic end of their history." Only in the holy writ is meaning no longer a "watershed" for the "flow of language and the flow of revelation."[2] The essay concludes with the suggestion that *all* great texts resemble holy texts, since their translatability inheres in them as a hidden potential. Implicit in this claim was a personal confession: Benjamin did not approach literature merely as a critic. Although it would be wrong to suggest that he saw all literature as sacred, he found in it a promise for meaning that overflows all languages and limits. A translator is like a secular prophet: he has the duty to free that meaning from its provincial boundaries and dispatch its gospel to all corners of the earth.

His efforts in translating texts from French to German were prodigious. In July 1925 he had signed with a publisher to produce a new translation of several volumes of Marcel Proust's *À la recherche du temps perdu*, a task for which he was promised 2,300 marks with the agreement that it would be completed by March of the following year. Although the compensation was hardly generous, it was "tolerable enough" to justify his taking on what he admitted would be "enormous work." He also translated "Anabase," the celebrated 1924 poem by Saint-John Perse. According to a provisional plan with the German publisher Insel Verlag, the poet Rainer Maria Rilke had initially agreed to undertake the translation himself, but, thanks to a recommendation from Hofmannsthal, the task was passed along to Benjamin. Rilke was expected to write a preface, but unfortunately the entire project came to naught, and the volume never appeared.[3] Benjamin also established a relationship with Willi Haas, the editor of the prestigious journal *Die Literarische Welt*, for whom he agreed to write "a regular column on new French art theory."[4] Haas, born into the Jewish community in Czechoslovakia, had once belonged to the Prague Circle that included writers such as Franz Kafka, Max Brod, and Franz Werfel. Benjamin's bond with the journal proved enormously important, and he succeeded in publishing more than one hundred essays there until Haas was forced to emigrate in 1933.[5] During these years Benjamin also read widely, especially in French literature, from essays by Paul Valéry to what he called "dubious" works by the French surrealists Louis Aragon and André Bréton, including the latter's "Surrealist Manifesto" from 1924. His early opinion of surrealism was hardly favorable; in a brief fragment from 1925 he dismissed Aragon's prose poem *Une vague de rêves* as "dream-kitsch."[6]

Benjamin recorded his experiences of that summer's Italian journey in "Naples," an essay that, in its eye for detail and decay, may well rank among the most touching portraits of a city ever written. He was especially drawn to the profusion of Mediterranean goods for sale. "In the fish market, this seafaring people has created a marine sanctuary as grandiose as those of the Netherlands. Starfish, crayfish, cuttlefish from the gulf waters, which teem with creatures, cover the benches and are often devoured raw with a little lemon." Each stall and alleyway attracted his attention, as if it held the secret of a neglected magic. "The long passageway is favored. In a glass-roofed one, there is a toyshop (in which perfume and liqueur glasses are also on sale) that would hold its own beside fairy-tale galleries." It appeared as if each and every individual, no matter how indigent, had a role to play in the daily carnival. "Even the most wretched pauper is sovereign in the dim, dual awareness of participating, in all his destitution, in one of the pictures of Neapolitan street life that will never return, and of enjoying in all his poverty the leisure to follow the great panorama."[7] The little cityscape of Naples may seem a marginal topic in Benjamin's oeuvre, but it became for him an early exercise in how to read urban space. Even the covered passageways would make a return in his study of the Parisian arcades. Later that year the essay appeared in the *Frankfurter Zeitung*, the daily newspaper that became synonymous with the fate of Weimar liberalism; its feuilleton section published essays by some of the most recognized authors of the age, including Alfred Döblin, Siegfried Kracauer, Joseph Roth, and Stefan Zweig.

Benjamin spent a portion of October 1925 on the island of Capri, and then traveled onward to Riga to see Asja Lacis, whose contributions to proletarian theater and ties with the Soviet avant-garde would exert a powerful turn, both political and aesthetic.[8] Lacis, intellectually vibrant and also beautiful, had struck his heart. To his great disappointment, however, Benjamin found that she was far too busy with her theatrical duties in Riga to pay him much notice, let alone return his romantic affection.[9] A bitter memory of his visit there is recorded in *One-Way Street*, a kaleidoscopic tour of modern city life that he had begun to write in 1923 and had been slowly expanding over the years. In one brief section of the book, "Stereoscope," he describes Riga as a "blackish dwarftown" with a "dirty stone embankment" alongside the Dvina River.[10] The book was finally published in 1928, and it opens with a dedication: "This street is named Asja Lacis Street after her who as an engineer, cut it through the author."

Despite its title, *One-Way Street* is a work that forgoes any linear narrative; it fractures urban experience into a series of miniature scenes, each of which is announced by a title as if by a street sign. In "These Spaces for Rent," Benjamin records the decline of criticism as the medium of public advertising colonizes city life:

> Fools lament the decay of criticism. For its day is long past. Criticism is a matter of correct distancing. It was at home in a world where perspectives and prospects counted and where it was still possible to adopt a standpoint. Now things press too urgently on human society. The "unclouded," "innocent" eye has become a lie, perhaps the whole naïve mode of expression sheer incompetence. Today the most real, mercantile gaze into the heart of things is the advertisement. It tears down the stage upon which contemplation moved, and all but hits us between the eyes with things as a car, growing to gigantic proportions, careens at us out of a film screen.[11]

Experimental but finely wrought, the book marks a change in Benjamin's aesthetic and political alignment. Thanks in part to the strong influence of Lacis herself, Benjamin was now ready to shrug off the legacies of Romantic criticism to embrace a more modernist sensibility that reflected both *die neue Sachlichkeit* ("the new objectivity," an aesthetic style of coolness and restraint) and the Dada method of montage. Ernst Bloch called the book "a philosophy in the form of a revue."[12] It was also an exercise in reading urban space that prepared the way for later works such as *A Berlin Chronicle* and the never finished *Arcades Project*.

By early December, Benjamin was back in Berlin alongside Dora and Stefan, where the three celebrated Hanukkah, then

Dora's birthday, and then Christmas with his parents. In a letter to Scholem he confirmed that Stefan was "of course learning Hebrew," but he added that "not much is accomplished in his elective courses and the only thing he really likes are the Bible stories." Benjamin asked Scholem if he might recommend "a Jewish reader (with German text)" for Stefan's benefit. From this letter one glimpses a rare picture of Benjamin as a father. "I read aloud to him for a few hours, if not every day, then certainly every week and in doing so wander aimlessly through a fairy tale edifice, something urged upon us by our books. Instead of this, I would like to read Jewish history or stories to him, something that, in the first analysis, would also be more appealing to me." To entertain Stefan and his circle of friends for Hanukkah, Benjamin retrieved his old puppet theater (presumably his own childhood possession) and assisted behind the curtains to perform a "spectacular fairy play" by the Austrian playwright Ferdinand Raimund. The letter to Scholem is also noteworthy for a rare reference to Benjamin's brother Georg, a pediatrician who belonged to the communist circle in Berlin. Benjamin reports that Georg had also "trained" his fiancée (a friend of their sister Dora) to be a communist, and he added, with wry humor, that his new Christian in-laws would therefore have "a doubly bitter pill to swallow."[13]

Paris, Marseilles, Moscow

In March of 1926, Benjamin moved to Paris, chiefly to continue his collaborative work with Franz Hessel in producing a German translation of Proust's *À la recherche du temps perdu*. An accomplished translator, Hessel would soon become known for his book *Walking in Berlin* (first published in 1929 as *Spazieren in Berlin*), an engaging and accessible portrait of the city that inspired Benjamin's own works, including *One-Way Street*, *Berlin Childhood Around 1900*, and, most of all, his study of the Parisian arcades. It was partly thanks to Hessel that Benjamin turned his attention to the phenomenon of *flânerie*, the habit of aimless urban strolling that had so fascinated Baudelaire and became a dominant theme in his essay "The Painter of Modern Life" (1860–1863). Baudelaire had called the flâneur a "passionate observer," but this description does not fully convey the depth of the idea. The flâneur is many things at once—dandy, critic, and poet—who embodies a new mode of perception in which the urban landscape is fractured into countless moments of dissociated experience. What the flâneur observes while walking down the street became a model for later exponents of the aesthetic avant-garde. This experience of aimless wandering anticipated the device of montage later deployed by interwar artists such as Kurt Schwitters, filmmakers such as Sergei Eisenstein, and novelists such as Döblin and James Joyce.

The comparison to Joyce is perhaps most illuminating. Much of Joyce's *Ulysses* consists in a montage of Dublin life as experienced by Leopold Bloom, the half-Jewish protagonist whose peregrinations across the city are broken into episodes that recall, however obliquely, the journeys of Homer's epic hero. Bloom is at once outsider and everyman: he encapsulates in a single day all of the confusions and pleasures of modern life. Much like Bloom, Baudelaire's flâneur remains both the exemplar of modern experience but also its critic: he is a ragpicker who selects from the remnants of bourgeois culture small objects or episodes that serve as allegories for a half-ruined civilization.

Hessel's *Walking in Berlin* is only one work within a larger genre of urban studies that included montage-like novels such as Döblin's *Berlin Alexanderplatz* (1929) and films such as Walther Ruttmann's *Berlin: Symphony of a Metropolis* (1927). Benjamin, too, became a gifted contributor to this genre. In *One-Way Street* (1928) he employed montage to transcribe the experience of the flâneur as he strolls from one attraction to another, from the filling station to the planetarium. Its chapters do not unite into a single narrative. More spatial than temporal, they create a montage-like and fragmentary map of the city. Much like a child, the flâneur has a passion for collecting that resembles Benjamin's own literary practice:

> *Untidy child.* Each stone he finds, each flower he picks, and each butterfly he catches is already the start of a collection, and every single thing he owns makes up one great collection. In him this passion shows its true face, the stern Indian expression that lingers on, but with a dimmed and manic glow, in antiquarians, researchers, bibliomaniacs. Scarcely has he entered life than he is a hunter. He hunts the spirits whose trace he scents in things; between spirits and things, years pass in which his field of vision remains free of people. His life is like a dream: he knows nothing lasting.[14]

In developing the device of montage, Benjamin found that Berlin served as the first great object of his attention. Eventually, however, he turned to other cityscapes—Naples, Moscow, and, most of all, Paris.

Working with Hessel on the translation of Proust was by no means the only reason Benjamin felt drawn to Paris. He also meant to pursue the woman who had now captured his heart, the sculptor Jula Radt-Cohn, whom he knew from his early days as a student at the Kaiser Friedrich School. That Cohn was married did not seem to matter at all: Benjamin in love behaved as was his habit, suffering but persistent. Between Cohn and Hessel he still found time to take in the everyday wonders of the French capital. Throughout the spring of 1926 he stayed in "a clean and pleasant" room at the Hôtel du Midi in Montparnasse, and he "absorbed Paris right down to my fingertips."[15] In the evenings he would venture out to lectures or dine with friends; he met Joseph Roth, Ernst Bloch, and Jean Cocteau, whose play *Orphée* from 1926 he found "extraordinarily interesting."[16] He visited a dancehall "for men and women and for men among themselves"; he took in a Punch and Judy show, and frequented art galleries but also some unjuried shows, where he deemed the paintings to be "horrid." He attended a "surrealist soirée in a small private theater in Montmartre" but confessed that he found it "pitiful."[17] Although he was delighted to find streets that were lined with bookstores, he announced, with the seeming pride of an addict, that he had not bought a single book. Instead he forced himself to get up as early as possible to spend the morning hours immersed in translation.

In mid-July Benjamin received the tragic news that his father had suddenly died, and he returned for a month to Berlin. Relations with Emil had seldom been easy. Financial quarrels between father and son had begun not long after Walter's return from Bern, when his father had stipulated that any further support would require that Walter assume a post in a bank. To his friend Florens Christian Rang he complained that his parents were "extremely rigid in their way of thinking." Their "pronounced pettiness and need for control" had become "a torture devouring all of the energy I have to work."[18] He returned to Paris later that summer in low spirits.[19] In early September he traveled to Marseilles, where he joined Kracauer for a brief stay and then traveled eastward to the beachside town of Agay for some "peace and quiet." He took a two-hour trip to Aix-en-Provence and remarked on the beauty of the town, but added that he had watched a bullfight there, a spectacle that struck him as "rather pathetic."[20] He wrote to Scholem that his nerves were in a bad state: for at least two weeks he could hardly take pen in hand to write.[21] This condition was hardly unusual. Scholem once remarked that even in his youth Benjamin's persona was pervaded by a "profound sadness," and that much of the acumen of his writing was due to an intimate familiarity with "the nature of sorrow."[22] Dürer's *Melencolia I*, the image to which

Asja Lacis

he had devoted close analysis in the *Trauerspiel* study, was not merely an object of scholarly attention; it was also his double.

By mid-October he returned to his family home in Berlin, but in November he received a further blow: Asja Lacis had suffered a health crisis in Moscow.[23] Since their liaison in Capri in 1924, Benjamin had not ceased to pine for Lacis, a brilliant woman, educated in philosophy and psychology, who led a unique experiment in proletarian children's theater in Riga and Moscow. She had initiated the project in 1918, when she worked with Russian orphans who were traumatized by war. Lacis was already attached to an Austrian-Jewish theatrical director, Bernhard Reich, with whom she had a daughter. Benjamin, however, could not extinguish his feelings for Lacis, and when he heard the news of her collapse he rushed to Moscow as soon as he could. He received funding from *Die Kreatur* (the journal co-edited by Martin Buber), for which he had promised to write an essay on his journey. He would remain in Moscow for nearly two months, through the darkest phase of the Russian winter.

Benjamin suffered, however, not only from the cold but also from a more serious problem: he could not speak Russian. Lacis was preoccupied with her work and did little more than tolerate his attentions, so the task fell to Reich to serve as his guide. Despite his disorientation Benjamin pressed headlong into the task of trying to make sense of cultural life in the Soviet Union, at a moment when its experimental phase was coming to an end. "In Russia," he wrote, "the proletariat has really begun to take possession of bourgeois culture." In the Polytechnic Museum, he observed displays of the various pieces of industrial equipment that powered the new society. He learned of *Komsomoltsy*, or communist clubs, the "Pioneers," or communist groups for children who sported red neckties, and the "Octobrists" or "Wolves," which was "the name given to little babies from the moment they are able to point to the picture of Lenin."[24] As was his habit, he lavished his literary skill on everyday details: "the snow-covered, narrow alleys," "the soft jargon of the Jewish clothiers," and "the ragpickers, with sacks on their backs."

It was obvious that his overall impressions of the new state were not at all favorable. "Russia is today not only a class but also a caste state," he explained. "The social status of a citizen is determined not by the visible exterior of his existence—his clothes or living place—but exclusively by his relations to the party." The post-revolutionary phase of the New Economic Policy had yielded to official repression. "No one living abroad has any idea of the terrible social ostracism to which the NEP man is here subjected." Artists and intellectuals associated with the Russian avant-garde now found themselves under terrific pressure to conform: "the intellectual is above all a functionary, working in the departments of censorship, justice, and finance, and, if he survives, participating in work—which, however, in Russia means power." He lamented that the bourgeoisie had vanished, along with the cafés they had once populated. "Free trade and free intellect have been abolished." As Stalin tightened his grip, the entire phase of aesthetic experimentation in Soviet culture was coming to an end. "[The] constructivists, suprematists, abstractionists, who under War Communism placed their graphic propaganda at the service of the Revolution have long since been dismissed. Today, only banal clarity is demanded."[25] In the diary that he kept during his stay in Moscow, he described himself as a "left-wing outsider," for whom the prospect of joining the Communist party was more or less "inconceivable."[26]

On the Airwaves

By early February 1927, Benjamin was back in Berlin. After recovering from the flu, he was able to turn his attention to writing up the report on his experiences in the Soviet Union. In a letter to Buber he promised that his presentation would be "devoid of all theory." He meant to do little more than offer "a picture of the city of Moscow as it is at this very moment." But he hastened to add that "all factuality is already theory," a phrase that anticipates the method of collecting and montage that he would develop most of all in his project on the Paris arcades.[27] In March he found a new way to supplement his income: broadcasting on the radio. Thanks to his childhood friend Ernst Schoen, a musician and poet who was now employed at the Südwestdeutsche Rundfunk (the radio station in Frankfurt), Benjamin contributed some eighty broadcasts on the radio during the era when the medium was still in its infancy.

The very first radio transmission ever heard in Germany was broadcast at eight in the evening on October 29, 1923.[28] It lasted only a single hour; after that the station went silent. But the Berlin Funk-Stunde or "radio hour" soon extended its programming to half a day; its programs consisted chiefly in music, supplemented by an occasional lecture, a literary reading, or play. By 1924 regional broadcasting companies had stretched their electromagnetic waves to most of the major urban centers across Germany, though for several years after that their signals remained too feeble to reach beyond the farthest edges of the cities. The farmlands and forests remained mostly silent. In its initial years the radio was a luxury reserved almost exclusively to the urban middle class, since the costs were considerable. To listen to the wireless a household had to buy a *Detektor*, or receiver; then one had to pay the post office for a "license" to operate the receiver, and in addition there was a monthly fee. In popular memory we tend to imagine a family nestled in comfort before a single speaker as if around the family hearth. But the earliest radios were not elegant pieces of furniture for shared experience; they were exotic contraptions with exposed mechanisms and personal headphones that isolated each listener within a private auditory space. Only in the late 1920s did the household radio assume a more domestic form with a single loudspeaker that projected the transmissions into a shared room.

On March 23, 1927, the disembodied voice of "Dr. Walter Benjamin" floated on the airwaves into German homes for the very first time. He lectured on "Young Russian Poets," an edifying subject about which he could claim some familiarity thanks to his recent travels in the Soviet Union. To Scholem he wrote with some embarrassment of "piddling radio matters" and dismissed the work as having "no interest except in economic terms." But he was surely mistaken. Although it was by nature an ephemeral medium, radio broadcasting turned out to be congenial to his talents. It permitted him to explore nearly every facet of modern life without constraint and in a short format that liberated him from the duty to speak about more elevating topics such as Goethe or Proust. Following his 1927 debut, he continued his career as a critic on the air, and for several years he managed to scratch out a tolerable existence all the while hoping for grander things.

Among the most entertaining are those reports in which the everyday becomes exotic, or the modern is interlaced with nostalgia. In a broadcast from late 1929 or early 1930, Benjamin describes the market halls in Berlin that he had first visited as a child, where the smell of fish, cheese, flowers, raw meat, and fruit all intermingle under one roof, creating a "dim and woozy aroma" that complemented "the light seeping through murky panes of lead-framed glass." He does not ignore the smallest details. He notes "the stone floor, which is always awash with run-off or dishwater and feels like the cold and slippery bottom of the ocean." In another broadcast he revisits the history of the 1755 Lisbon earthquake, which sent tremors across the Mediterranean from the coasts of France to Morocco. Eighteenth-century Lisbon, a thriving hub of Portugal's global empire, at the time boasted not less than 250,000 inhabitants, of whom nearly a quarter perished. It was said that the cathedral towers in faraway Seville shook "like reeds in the wind." To be sure, Benjamin was only one in a long line of critics who wrote about the earthquake; European philosophers from Voltaire to Kant had pondered its meaning. But Benjamin possessed a skill in description that surpassed nearly all his predecessors, and in the brief twenty minutes of his broadcast he conveyed the terror of the event with inimitable precision. He ascribed special importance to the earthquake as a sign that the earth's crust is never at rest, that the ground beneath us is in "perpetual upheaval." Nature for Benjamin is transient, not eternal, and its history is no less violent than the history of humanity.

A similar theme recurs in one of his last broadcasts from the spring of 1932, a report on the Mississippi River flood of 1927 that claimed hundreds of lives in the precincts of New Orleans and plunged 100,000 square miles of farmland underwater, from Missouri to Kentucky to Tennessee. An estimated half a million inhabitants lost their homes. Benjamin paints for his listeners a portrait of three brothers who tried desperately to save their livestock but were forced to climb to the peak of their roof while the rising waters raged below. Only one of the brothers would survive, and Benjamin quotes a long passage from the man's harrowing experience.

With his characteristic habit of interpretation, Benjamin turns the flood into a political allegory. Just before he bids farewell to his radio audience, he promises that he is not yet done with the Mississippi: "On some other occasion we'll return to its banks during times when the river flowed peacefully in its bed, but there was little peace to be found on its shores." In a veiled reference to the Ku Klux Klan, he explains that "we'll find ourselves on the banks of the Mississippi, but this time facing the raging elements of human cruelty." Listeners alert to his unstated analogy would have recognized that this was not only an allusion to North America. "The dams that the law has built to contain them have held up no better than the actual ones made from earth and stone." Just a year before the Nazi seizure of power, Benjamin was also alluding to political conditions at home, expressing his fear that human institutions might not suffice to hold back the flood.

The flood finally came. In the years before his final departure from Germany, Benjamin had collected an anthology of letters for the *Frankfurter Zeitung* under the pseudonym "Detlef Holz." The series, perhaps originally planned for the radio, was later published in Switzerland as a book, *German Men and Women* (*Deutsche Menschen*); but this was in 1936, when Benjamin had definitively left the country of his birth. The letters, written by authors such as Kant, Goethe, Schlegel, and Friedrich Schleiermacher, all date to the late eighteenth and early nineteenth centuries, and taken together they may seem little more than an exercise in literary history. In retrospect, however, the anthology appears as a loving tribute to the German writers whose works Benjamin most cherished. By the time the book was published, he was living in Paris and the book became a kind of memorial to the rapidly vanishing ideals of the Enlightenment. Benjamin sent a copy of the book to Scholem, inscribed with a personal dedication. "Gerhard, you may find a chamber for the memories of your youth in this ark I built, when the fascist deluge began to rise. January 1937 Walter."[29]

Hebrew Lessons

Given the uncertainty of his prospects for a career in Germany, it is hardly surprising that Benjamin began to entertain overtures from Gershom Scholem that he secure a teaching post of some kind in Jerusalem, where Scholem and his wife Escha had lived since their emigration in 1923. On numerous occasions Scholem had urged Benjamin to begin his study of Hebrew, but Benjamin always demurred, explaining that various more pressing obligations first had to be completed. In 1927, however, Benjamin agreed to Scholem's proposal that they meet in Paris with Judah Magnes, an American-born rabbi with degrees from Berlin and Heidelberg, who had emigrated to Palestine in 1922 and was now serving as the first chancellor of the Hebrew University in Jerusalem.[30] The meeting lasted for two hours, during which time Benjamin expressed his wish "to approach the great texts of Jewish literature through the medium of the Hebrew language, not as a philologist but as a metaphysician." He also declared "his readiness to come to Jerusalem, whether on a temporary or a permanent basis."[31]

Benjamin was evidently eager to prove both his intellectual credentials and his personal sincerity. In Scholem's recollection, he explained that he realized that "his ideas on the philosophy of language could not find their focus in the German and French literature accessible to him." He added that his friendship with Scholem had helped him to see that "his focal point" would consist in "an occupation with the Hebrew language and literature." He explained that it was most of all his work as a translator that had moved him toward "philosophical and theological reflections" that could only be resolved with "his immersion in Hebrew." He added that these matters had also "made him ever more clearly conscious of his Jewish identity."[32]

For a scholar who until this point in his life had concerned himself almost exclusively with German and French literature, such a statement may strike us as implausible. The shift of topics would have required not only an abrupt turn in his intellectual path; it would have also demanded that he confront the manifold challenges of fashioning a new existence for himself beyond the bourgeois comforts of city life in Europe. Scholem had informed him of plans in Jerusalem to found a school for the humanities, and in his current circumstances Benjamin must have felt especially motivated to present himself as a worthy candidate. In his memoir Scholem recalls his own feelings of surprise at the certainty with which his friend declared his intentions. "Never before had Benjamin placed himself so decisively in this context, nor did he do so on any subsequent occasion." Although no firm agreement was made, Benjamin proposed that he visit Jerusalem for one year to improve his Hebrew, perhaps in the summer or fall of 1928. Meanwhile, Magnes promised to give the proposal all due consideration. In Scholem's recollection Benjamin was "ecstatic."[33]

The coming years would show, however, that despite his apparent enthusiasm and good intentions Benjamin had neither the will nor the intellectual drive to transform his plans into a reality. To Scholem he confessed that he was a mere *Amhoorez* [*sic*], the Hebrew word for an untutored Jew. He also asked if Scholem might recommend a Hebrew teacher, and once again pressed for details regarding the financial terms of his Jerusa-

Passport photo of Walter Benjamin, circa 1928

lem visit.[34] In June 1928, Magnes passed through Berlin and was able to spare a half hour to discuss the proposal with Benjamin in more detail. Although in his official capacity as rector, Magnes could commit neither funds nor a scholarly position to Benjamin for his stay in Jerusalem, he assured Benjamin that his letters of support were strong. In all likelihood something would be created for him at the institute for the humanities once it was officially opened, perhaps in the coming two years. Meanwhile Magnes was able to offer a stipend to study Hebrew, and he suggested that Benjamin should speak with the esteemed rabbi Leo Baeck (who then lived in Berlin) about his plans.[35]

By late August Benjamin wrote in good humor to Scholem: "My trip to Palestine is a settled matter, as is my intention to strictly observe the course of study prescribed by Your hierosolymitanischen [Jerusalemite] Excellency. Let me moreover avow that the awestruck undersigned will be able to read the alphabet common to the country before he sets foot on the soil of erez isroel."[36]

The timing, however, never seemed quite right. In June 1928 his mother suffered a stroke that severely impaired her speech, and Benjamin felt obliged to remain by her side. He explained that his arrival in Jerusalem would be delayed at least until the end of the year. He also felt he had to make further headway on his new study of the Paris arcades. From Magnes he received a stipend of more than three thousand marks to support his Hebrew lessons; and at the end of the month he announced to Scholem, "My way is clear to begin Hebrew lessons," though he noted that it would "affect my work on the Arcades." He added that he now expected to come to Jerusalem "in the spring of next year."[37] On February 14, 1929, however, he wrote again to Scholem with a somewhat sheepish apology: "I am now putting off my arrival for a second time and have to reckon with the danger of your no longer taking me seriously," though he added that there was "no other course but for me to begin immediately with the study of Hebrew in Berlin." It was now his plan to defer his visit to Palestine to the fall; his mother's condition had grown far worse and he feared that she might be nearing the end. Meanwhile he pursued other options that would not require long-distance travel. A conversation with Martin Buber raised the possibility that he might be recommended to lecture at the "School for Jewish Youth" in Berlin. But Benjamin confessed he did not feel qualified for such a position. "I more easily see myself sitting at one of its desks than standing at the rostrum."[38]

This pattern, of plans made and plans deferred, would continue for several years. Benjamin's hesitation clearly placed Scholem in an awkward position, since he had advocated for his friend with colleagues in Jerusalem. In a remarkable letter from the end of February 1930 Scholem finally vented his frustration. "Three years ago you thought, and I agreed, that you had gotten to the point where a productive confrontation with Judaism seemed the only way of making real progress in your work." This no longer appeared plausible. "It is evident," wrote Scholem, "that the opinion you expressed three years ago has been revealed to be exaggerated and wrong." Clearly Benjamin did not see "taking the path of Hebrew" as in any sense inevitable. Scholem asked his friend to explain himself with candor, and he promised that "the divergencies in our autobiographies" would not lead to "personal apocalypse" if Benjamin were to "reveal that you can no longer, and will no longer, in this life consider a true confrontation with Judaism."[39]

In April 1930 Benjamin responded. "I must once again put off giving a definitive answer to the question it asks." His letter reads as both a litany of excuses and personal confession: "I have come to know living Judaism in absolutely no form other than you. The question of my relationship to Judaism is always the question of how I stand . . . in relation to the forces you have touched in me." He acknowledged that he had been guilty of "procrastination," that it had been "stretched to the limit." The habit of delay had become "second nature to me when it comes to the most important situations in my life." But he asked Scholem for forbearance as he tried to loosen the "extremely tangled knot" that tied him to his life in Berlin. After painful legal disputes, in the spring of 1930 Benjamin and Dora had at last finalized their divorce, and in early November his mother passed away after a long and severe illness.[40] He now felt that he was confronted with the task of starting a "new life" after the previous one had collapsed. "Everything is coming down to a decision that cannot be put off much longer." He added that he would visit Palestine "before the end of the year."[41] He had made the very same promise many times, but it was one that he would never fulfill.

A Frankfurt Friendship

Even while Scholem was seeking to draw him in one direction, Benjamin had forged a separate friendship with Theodor W. Adorno that pulled him in another. He had first made the acquaintance of Adorno briefly in 1923 in Frankfurt, and then came to know him somewhat better in 1925 when they traveled together with Siegfried Kracauer in Naples.[42] But a genuine friendship did not actually develop between the two until February 1928, when Adorno came to visit Berlin. The relationship between them grew stronger from that point onward, though it was always troubled by intellectual disagreement and suppressed feelings of both rivalry and resentment that neither of them could fully extinguish. All the same, their friendship proved to be one of the most enduring and fruitful bonds in their lives.

Born in 1903, Adorno was younger than Benjamin by eleven years and, not unlike Benjamin, he had grown up in a well-to-do middle-class home. Unlike Benjamin, however, Adorno was raised without any real sense of affiliation with Judaism. His father, Oscar Wiesengrund, a wine merchant in Frankfurt, was of Jewish descent but had officially separated himself from the Jewish community; his mother, Maria Calvelli-Adorno, was an opera singer from an Italian Catholic family, and following her wishes their son was baptized as a Catholic, but later confirmed as a Protestant. Later in his life Adorno (whom Benjamin addressed in correspondence up through 1936 as "Herr Wiesengrund," before switching to "Teddie") would adopt his mother's last name, chiefly out of a sense of strongly felt affinity with her musical side of the family. Suspicions that he adopted the Italianate surname out of a desire to suppress his Jewish heritage are lacking in evidence. In any event, his maternal surname did little to protect him from discrimination. After the passage of the Nazis' "racial" laws Adorno had to abandon his hopes for an academic career in Germany. Many years later, he seems to have suffered a painful sense of guilt. In *Negative Dialectics*, the dense and difficult magnum opus of philosophy that he published in 1966, he wrote of the feeling that plagues many survivors. Although written in the third person, one can discern a personal allusion to his late friend:

> . . . it is not wrong to raise the less cultural question whether after Auschwitz you can go on living—especially whether one who escaped by accident, one who by rights should have been killed, may go on living. . . . As compensation he will be haunted by dreams such as that he is no longer living at all, that he was gassed in 1944 and his whole existence since then has been only in his imagination, an emanation of the mistaken wish of a man killed twenty years earlier.[43]

Passages such as this one bring to the surface the sense of personal and intellectual debt that bound Adorno to Benjamin. Well after he received word of what had happened in the Pyrenees, Adorno continued to argue with his friend over questions of aesthetics and philosophy, honoring his memory while also contesting his claims.[44]

Unlike Benjamin, Adorno moved without much difficulty up the academic ladder in the German university system. In 1924 he received his doctorate in Frankfurt with a dissertation on Husserlian phenomenology that he had written under the direction of Hans Cornelius (the same professor who declined Benjamin's habilitation the following year). Adorno's initial effort to submit a thesis on psychoanalysis for the habilitation had been denied, but he later succeeded in securing his habilitation with a thesis on Kierkegaard, which he submitted to the theologian Paul Tillich in 1931. When it came to aesthetic matters,

Adorno and Benjamin shared in common a strong interest in literature. But Adorno possessed neither his friend's knowledge of literary history nor his extraordinary gift for the interpretation of literary imagery and metaphor. On the other hand, Adorno had a stronger, more systematic training in the philosophical tradition. He was also an accomplished musician and had studied composition with Alban Berg in Vienna. His understanding of music was deep but not wide; when confronted with popular forms of music or culture he tended to respond with incomprehension verging on disdain. This sharply distinguished him from Benjamin, who was more fascinated by the prospects for human perception introduced into culture with the new technologies of photography and film.

These differences, in both acumen and temperament, became more consequential with the passage of time. In 1928, however, the two men initiated a regular correspondence and found that they shared many interests in common. Around this same time, Adorno was developing an affiliation with the Institute for Social Research, the neo-Marxist and multidisciplinary organization associated with the University of Frankfurt. This affiliation only grew stronger in early 1931, when the position of serving as the institute's director passed into the hands of Max Horkheimer, a philosopher who, like Adorno, had written his dissertation at Frankfurt with Hans Cornelius. Since Horkheimer always looked upon Benjamin with some skepticism, Benjamin never felt himself wholly accepted into the institute's inner circle. His friendship with Adorno, too, was at times strained by their differences in status. Adorno was younger but relatively successful, while Benjamin found himself living in a state of some financial precarity.[45]

These differences, however, did not prevent the development of a friendship between Adorno and Benjamin, even if their relationship was never wholly free of tension and misunderstanding. When Adorno's habilitation on Kierkegaard was published as a book in 1933, Scholem thought he could discern themes that had been borrowed without proper acknowledgment from Benjamin's study of the *Trauerspiel.* In a letter to Benjamin he characterized the book as "a sublime plagiarism of your thought" and "uncommon chutzpah."[46] The accusation, however, seems rather misplaced. In what seems to have been a good faith effort to honor Benjamin's work despite its official rejection by the university faculty, Adorno conducted a seminar at Frankfurt on the *Trauerspiel* book. In fact he offered the seminar twice, first in the late spring or early summer of 1932 and once again the following autumn. With apparent bitterness, though, Benjamin reported that Adorno had not indicated the use of the book in the university course catalogue. The reasons for this omission are unknown.[47]

Despite these tensions, the friendship with Adorno and his growing affiliation with the Institute for Social Research were to play an important role in turning Benjamin toward strategies of interpretation that were broadly Marxist, or, at the very least, *marxisant.* His attention to the philosophical aspects of historical materialism was first awakened as early as 1923, when he became familiar with *History and Class Consciousness*, a pathbreaking exercise in Hegelian Marxism interpretation by Georg Lukács. In a letter from 1924 Benjamin wrote that the book "astonished me because these principles resonate for me or validate my own thinking." The book also stimulated his interest in what he ventured to call "the political practice of communism." All the same, his own philosophical orientation was never truly Marxist in the orthodox sense. Although he fell under the influence of friends with a strongly Marxist orientation such as Bloch, Bertolt Brecht, and Lacis, he never overcame a certain skepticism regarding the deeper principles of official Marxist doctrine. Even the more subtle thinkers in the Marxist tradition, after all, understood history as the theater for the gradual unfolding of human freedom. But this was a vision of immanent historical change that Benjamin could not fully endorse.

In a letter to Scholem in 1924 he explained why even the more sophisticated strands of Marxist theory left him unconvinced. Lukács's *History and Class Consciousness* had been published only a year earlier, and he had not found the time to read it with care. But he already suspected that the book demanded philosophical commitments that he could not accept. "I would be surprised," he wrote, "if the foundations of my nihilism were not to manifest themselves against communism in an antagonistic confrontation with the concepts and assertions of Hegelian dialectics."[48] The statement is highly revealing, almost a confession. Benjamin no doubt found certain motifs in Marxism stimulating, but there was at the core of his thinking an untamed, even untamable spirit that could not be contained with any logical system. The Hegelian dialectic expresses an unbounded confidence in the rationality that governs the world, and in Marxism, too, this key tenet of the dialectic survives. But this was a premise Benjmain could hardly accept without doing violence to his deepest instincts. He was too much in the grips of what he called his "nihilism," a spirit of anarchic romanticism essentially at odds with all systematic philosophy. By the end of his life, he would compose an essay on the concept of history in which his antagonism to the Hegelian idea of historical reason became altogether plain. But this final reckoning still lay several years in the future.

Some of Benjamin's closest friends did not welcome his apparent flirtations with Marxist theory. In a remarkable letter from March 1931, Scholem expressed his fear that Benjamin was in danger of losing his bearings. He accused Benjamin of "a singularly intensive kind of self-deception" and wrote of "an astonishing incompatibility" between his "*real*" and his "*pretended* modes of thought." If it was even plausible to say that Benjamin had adopted some species of historical materialism, the result verged on philosophical incoherence. "You gain your insights," Scholem wrote, "not through strict application of a materialistic method but quite independently of it (at best) or (at worst, as in some writings of the last two years) by playing with the ambiguities and dissonances of this method."[49] Whether Scholem was right to accuse Benjamin of inconsistencies remains a matter of fierce debate. But Scholem had other reasons to be anxious. His own brother Werner had opted to join the communist movement, and had become a leading figure in the KPD (or Communist Party of Germany); in the mid-'20s Werner even served as an official communist representative in the *Reichstag*. In 1926, however, he had been expelled from the party due to his vocal condemnation of the Soviet Union for its persecution of the United Left Opposition (a faction associated with Leon Trotsky and Grigory Zinoviev that opposed Stalin).[50] The example of his brother Werner must have weighed heavily on his mind when Scholem admonished Benjamin to keep his distance from the communist movement. He speculated about "what would happen to your writings if you were ever . . . to publish them *within* the Communist party, and this prospect is quite dismal." Catastrophe would surely ensue, he warned, once "your fellow dialecticians unmasked you as a typical counterrevolutionary and bourgeois—something that would be inevitable."[51]

Such warnings, of course, must be taken with more than a few grains of salt. After all, Scholem was hardly a disinterested party. He placed the greatest value on those features in Benjamin's work that demonstrated some devotion to Judaism (or, at least, to Jewish themes) and the vigor with which he urged Benjamin to learn Hebrew and move to Jerusalem was only the most obvious sign of his investment, both political and intellectual, in his friend's future path. To understand why Scholem felt such anxiety about his friend's flirtations with Marxism, one must keep in mind that Scholem saw Benjamin as a thinker torn between two angels, one menacing, the other a trustworthy guide. In April 1931 Benjamin responded to Scholem with an explanation. He harbored not the "slightest illusions" concerning the hostile reception that his work would find in the communist sphere, but he could not agree with Scholem's unstated premise that there were only two options—either Judaism or total capitulation to the Communist party. Benjamin alone would decide the meaning of his ideas. Ironically, Scholem seemed to grant this authority to the party. Benjamin admitted that he was hardly a communist in the orthodox sense. But it was far more important to ensure that nothing in his work be vulnerable to the forces of the counterrevolution:

> Do you want to prevent me from hanging a red flag out of my window, saying that it is only a little piece of cloth? If someone produces "counterrevolutionary" writings, as you quite correctly characterize mine *from the Party's point of view*, should he also expressly place them at the disposal of the counterrevolution? Should he not, rather, denature them, like ethyl alcohol, and make them definitely and reliably unusable for the counterrevolution at the risk that no one will be able to use them?[52]

Behind this disagreement lay a further reason that Scholem could not fully acknowledge or accept. For Benjamin as for many others in the interwar period, an intellectual interest in Marxism did not necessarily imply a commitment to the communist movement or the Communist party. On the contrary; at the moment in the late 1920s when Benjamin was strengthening his intellectual ties with Adorno and the circle of left-wing intellectuals associated with the institute in Frankfurt, he was only one participant among the many who were following the examples of Lukács and Bloch: they were turning to Marxism not as the rigid doctrine of the Communist party but as a philosophically labile framework of interpretation that kept its distance from formal party affiliations. Lukács himself, much to his discredit, would soon succumb to the party authorities and even recant his most original contributions to Marxist theory. Benjamin, however, despite his occasional flirtations with the idea of communism, never took the move of actually joining the Communist party. Much like Zionism, communism remained for him mostly an *idea*, a vehicle of utopian aspiration that had only the most tenuous connection to worldly events.

In 1928 Benjamin wrote to Siegfried Kracauer, "Wiesengrund and I have been together often and fruitfully."[53] Around this time, apparently at Adorno's recommendation, Benjamin also began reading more deeply in contemporary Marxist theory. His studies included Karl Korsch's *Marxism and Philosophy* (published in 1923), a work that, alongside Lukács's *History and Class Consciousness* (also published in 1923), helped to elevate Marxism to new heights of philosophical nuance and pointed the way toward what Max Horkheimer, as director of the Institute for Social Research, would call "critical theory."[54]

In May 1931, Adorno gave his inaugural lecture as professor, "The Actuality of Philosophy," at the University of Frankfurt, and he passed along manuscript copies to Benjamin, Kracauer, and Bloch. Benjamin responded more or less favorably, writing to Adorno that "the piece as a whole succeeds in its aim [and] that in its very concision it presents an extremely penetrating articulation of the most essential ideas which we share." He took care to note that a genuinely philosophical approach to Marxism meant sustaining a critical posture regarding its claims rather than treating it as a settled doctrine. But he could not resist offering a few notes of criticism regarding Adorno's lecture: "I think Bloch is right to claim that the connection between materialism and the ideas in question seems forced in places, but this is fully justified by the spiritual climate and can probably be defended wherever it is a question not simply of 'applying' Marxism like a coat of fresh paint, but rather of working with it, and that means, for all of us, *struggling* with it." For Benjamin, Marxist theory would not serve as an unquestioned habitat or fixed ground. Even Jacob, after all, had wrestled with the angel and had not perished. And Marxism, not unlike Judaism, was an intellectual inheritance with which he could contend without destroying himself. On a less comfortable note, Benjamin insinuated that in the lecture Adorno had borrowed a key idea from him but without acknowledgment: Adorno declared that the task of philosophy was "to interpret the intentionless character of reality." Benjamin had expressed the very same thought some years earlier in his study of the *Trauerspiel*.[55]

Reading Kafka

Over the coming years Adorno and Benjamin would often recognize that they shared many ideas in common. Among the more striking cases is their readings of Kafka, whose novels *The Trial* and *The Castle* were published posthumously (in 1925 and 1926, respectively). Their publication aroused some controversy, since his friend Max Brod had disobeyed the author's express instructions that the novels be destroyed. But most critics were more interested in the content of Kafka's works. Benjamin's earliest essay on Kafka appeared in *Die Literarische Welt* in late November 1929. Though relatively brief, the essay extols Kafka as an author whose "shattering" work confronts the "darkest matters of human life." To read Kafka, Benjamin writes, is to plunge into questions that have typically preoccupied theologians and only seldom poets.[56] Five years later, Benjamin wrote a far more sustained essay on Kafka in order to mark the tenth anniversary of the author's death.[57] Published in the *Jüdische Rundschau* in 1934, it ranks among his most masterful feats of interpretation.

Kafka's fictional universe, Benjamin writes, is a "world of offices and registries, of musty, shabby, dark rooms." And the figures who populate this world are no less enigmatic than the world itself. "No matter how highly placed they may be, they are always fallen or falling men, although even the lowest and seediest of them, the doorkeepers and decrepit officials, may abruptly and strikingly appear in the fullness of their power." An exemplary case is the father in the short story "The Judgement," a bedridden and seemingly senile old man who, as if throwing off a "cosmic burden," suddenly rises from his bed and "sentences his son to death by drowning." Once again Benjamin seems troubled by a symbolic knot between mortality and water: the death of the son recalls the death of Ottilie in Goethe's *Elective Affinities.* But Kafka's stories are less concerned with specifics of personality or place. For Benjamin they evoke an archaic, pre-biblical age, "beyond the time of the giving of the Law on twelve tablets." Kafka knows that the law would signify a victory over this prehistorical world, but the law remains inaccessible and unintelligible. "In Kafka the written law is contained in lawbooks, but these are secret; by basing itself on them, the prehistoric world exerts its rule all the more ruthlessly." Kafka's prose pieces are somehow eccentric to the tradition of Western literature: they have "a relationship to religious teaching [*zur Lehre*] similar to the one Haggadah has to Halachah." They are not parables, Benjamin insists, yet all the same they cannot be taken at face value. We are left with the impression that the religious revelation to which these stories may refer does not exist at all. "Kafka might have said that these are relics transmitting the teachings, although we could just as well regard them as precursors preparing the teachings."[58]

Benjamin brings his most powerful insights to bear on the question of Kafka's relationship with Judaism. Citing Willy Haas (Kafka's acquaintance from the Prague circle and the founder of *Die Literarische Welt*), Benjamin admits that the "mysterious center" of Kafka's work "derives from the Jewish religion." But the connection to Judaism is hardly simple. Kafka may know the religious truth that "the gate to justice is study," but unlike his Jewish ancestors "Kafka doesn't dare attach to this study the promises which tradition has attached to the study of the Torah. His assistants are sextons who have lost their house of prayer; his students are pupils who have lost the Holy Writ [*Schrift*]." Unlike Haas and Brod, who underscore Kafka's debts to Judaism, Benjamin finds in Kafka's writing the traces of an animistic and prehistorical world that *precedes* monotheism. The strange animals that inhabit his tales—Josephine the mouse singer, the unnamed creature in "The Burrow," the chimera-like "Cat-Lamb," or the hunter Gracchus who turns into a butterfly—all belong to "the great herd" that in Kafka's world signify "the strangeness of our body." Perhaps most striking of all is Odradek, the fantastical creature who appears in Kafka's short story "The Cares of a Family Man." Half animal, half object, Odradek resembles a star-shaped spool, around which are a few broken pieces of knotted thread, while a small rod fixed at right angles enables it to stand upright as if on two legs. It seldom makes its appearance and prefers to hide, in the attic or other places of "discarded, forgotten objects." Benjamin sees this creature as "the most singular bastard which the prehistorical world has begotten with guilt." Odradek, he concludes, is "the form which things assume in oblivion."[59]

In this interpretation, Benjamin places its greatest emphasis on a theme that he had explored in his study of the *Trauerspiel:* the theme of fallen and distorted nature. Creatures from the mythic or supernatural world appear frequently in Kafka's work—consider, for instance, the parable "The Silence of the Sirens"—and they have little or no power to escape their fallen condition. But this is what makes them so troubling. Kafka has refashioned the old legends and myths into what Benjamin calls "fairy tales for dialecticians." The stories convey the grim lesson that Kafka once related in a conversation with Max Brod, that "our world is only a bad mood of God." Brod had responded,

"Then there is hope outside this manifestation of the world that we know." To this Kafka offered a wry retort: "Oh, plenty of hope, an infinite amount of hope—but not for us."[60]

In a letter to Benjamin, Adorno expressed his "overwhelming sense of gratitude" for the Kafka essay. The essay showed once again how much they shared in common, especially concerning "the image of theology." In Benjamin's essay Adorno felt that he could discern the very same idea that he had explored in his study of Kierkegaard, namely, that theological matters can appear only in an oblique or "inverted" form. Kafka was not a genuine theologian (as his friend Max Brod had claimed). He was a this-worldly critic who made use of theological concepts only to reveal the world in all its destitution and ruin. By means of inversion, Kafka furnished the reader with "a photograph of our earthly life from the perspective of a redeemed life."[61] For Benjamin this idea struck a chord of recognition. As early as 1920 or 1921 in the "Theological-Political Fragment," he had been fascinated with the image of this-worldly destitution. The *Trauerspiel* study had explored a similar idea. Within the fallen world there is no redemption; grace comes from God alone. The only force strong enough to break the mythic illusions of secular history was to be found beyond history, in the realm of the "messianic."

By the early 1930s Benjamin saw all too many reasons to despair over the course of history. With the Nazi seizure of power in January 1933, changes both large and small proved that Germany was no longer a safe home for Jews or for anyone on the political left. Benjamin reported bitterly to Scholem that "the air is hardly fit to breathe anymore—a condition which of course loses significance as one is being strangled anyway."[62] At the *Frankfurter Zeitung*, the left-liberal newspaper where Benjamin had published so many of his essays, the editor of the feuilleton page was removed from his post. He described the new atmosphere of suspicion, in which "you look first at people's lapels and after that usually do not want to look them in the face anymore."[63] The flood had come. In May he received the news that the police had arrested his brother Georg, who was then sent onward to the concentration camp run by the Sturmabteilung in Sonnenburg.[64] He raised a "few hundred marks" that would make it possible for him to live on the island of Ibiza. On March 17, 1933, Benjamin left Germany for the very last time to begin a new phase of life abroad.

6

Paris Years

Paris was in many respects his adopted home. Like Heinrich Heine and Karl Marx the century before, and like so many German and Jewish refugees from fascism in the 1930s, Benjamin found in Paris a community of intellectuals and artists who shared not only a common language and cultural inheritance but also common fears about the rising tide of political reaction. Among his new acquaintances were the political theorist Hannah Arendt and the photographer Gisèle Freund, both of whom became friends. There were also familial ties. The philosopher Günther Anders (Arendt's first husband, born Günther Stern) was in fact Benjamin's cousin.[1] To be sure, Paris was hardly unknown terrain: he had traveled there several times in the 1920s, and he possessed a facility in French that made him a virtual native. No one who lacked such formidable linguistic skill could have undertaken translations of Proust. In his "Paris Diary," written for *Die Literarische Welt* in 1930, he had written:

"No sooner do you arrive in the city than you feel rewarded. The resolve not to write about it is futile. You reconstruct the preceding day just like children who reconstruct the table full of presents on Christmas Day."[2] As early as 1928 his love of wandering the Parisian streets had awakened in him the idea of composing an essay that he provisionally called "Paris Arcades: A Dialectical Fairy Play." For the time being he saw the project as "extremely precarious," though he hoped that it might fulfill a cycle of writings on French culture just as the *Trauerspiel* book had completed a cycle on German themes.[3]

The Villa Verde and Ibiza

Paris was not the only possibility that he considered for refuge, but where else could he make a living? In February 1933 he had written to Scholem: "There are places where I could earn a minimal income, and places where I could live on a minimal income, but not a single place where these two conditions coincide."[4] Regarding the prospect for emigration to Palestine, Scholem was compelled to be honest. He told Benjamin in no uncertain terms that his chance of making a living there was now a "clear impossibility." But he hastened to add that as a place of refuge "circumstances . . . are basically favorable, even if only for a more or less limited time."[5] By mid-April, however, the stream of European refugees had become a torrent. "Here in Palestine there is a tremendous commotion," Scholem wrote. "Every ship brings hundreds of people from Germany, conveying a harrowing picture of the medieval events. Ever since the mass exodus of many thousands of people on March 30 and April 1, telegrams from all possible relatives and friends . . . have been raining down like hail, left and right, and you can see from them how almost everybody took off headlong and especially how, apparently, anybody who is remotely able to do so is taking his children out of this new hell."[6]

Benjamin's deepest worries were for his family. As late as May 1933, his ex-wife Dora and their son Stefan were still living in Germany, but by the fall of 1934 Dora had at last moved abroad. She ended up in San Remo, Italy, where she opened a boarding house called the Villa Verde.[7] Stefan would remain in Berlin for some years, despite Walter's plea that Dora try to send him off to live with her brother in Palestine.[8] Eventually Stefan moved, first to Vienna, and then to San Remo in 1937. But he could not stay there long. Lacking citizenship, he was deported in 1941 from Italy to Australia; he survived the war and became an antiquarian bookseller in London, where he remained until his death in 1971.[9] Benjamin was also wracked with anxiety for his brother and sister. In the spring of 1933, Georg had been imprisoned for his political activities; his sister Dora remained through the year in Germany, but she also owned an apartment in Paris and fled there by 1934.[10]

Benjamin arrived in Paris on March 19, 1933, but stayed only a brief while before he traveled onward to Ibiza, the Spanish island he had visited the previous year. Relatively unknown to tourists at the time, the rocky, radiant island was a place of poverty, though it was thickly populated with fig trees and goats. During his first sojourn there in the spring of 1932 he wrote in a playful mood to Gretel Karplus (later Adorno's wife) that he was forced to do without the assorted necessities of urban existence, such as "electric light and butter, liquor and running water, flirting and reading the paper."[11] That year he also made the acquaintance of the art historian Jean Selz, who would later publish a portrait of Benjamin during his island stay:

> Benjamin had difficulty walking: he couldn't go very fast, but was able to walk for long periods of time. The long walks we took together through the rolling countryside, among carob, almonds, and pine trees, were made even longer by our conversations, which constantly forced him to stop. He admitted that walking kept him from thinking. Whenever some-

> thing interested him he would say, "Tiens, tiens!" [Wait, wait!] This was the signal that he was about to think, and therefore stop. There were times when he said, "So, so," as if speaking to himself, but usually it was "Tiens, tiens," even while speaking German with other Germans, the younger and less respectful of whom nicknamed him Tiens-tiens as a result.[12]

The following year, when Benjamin returned to the island, the atmosphere in the town of San Antonio had changed. He was no longer a visitor but a refugee; he was prone to bouts of depression and was unusually sensitive to noise. Much to his dismay, he found that developers had started their work with "blastings and hammer blows," and even the cheapest residences were becoming too costly for a foreign intellectual of limited means.[13] However, despite news of the worsening political situation on the European mainland, he managed to find small moments of respite. In a June 1933 letter to Gretel Karplus he described his daily routine: he would wake up at half past six or seven in the morning and then climb the hillside to a spot where he had hidden his deck chair in the brush. There he would read, sometimes detective stories by Georges Simenon. Thanks to a small shipment of books from Max Horkheimer, he also read Louis-Ferdinand Céline's novel *Voyage to the End of the Night* (first published in French the previous year). When taking a short stroll through the forest he would think of Paris. After lunch, when the Mediterranean sun grew too strong for serious reading or writing, he would surrender to his fatigue and take a nap. On the shoreline he could watch the lobstermen go about their daily work, and he also made friends with the grandson of the painter Paul Gauguin, a taciturn man who accompanied him on walks to the inland mountains. In the evenings he might play dominos or chess, and by half past nine he would go to bed, perhaps reading a bit more by candlelight.[14]

During the later summer, with assistance from Jean Selz, Benjamin made progress on a French translation of his mem-

Walter Benjamin in San Antonio, Ibiza, 1932. Also pictured: Jean Selz, Paul René Gaugin, and the fisherman Tomàs Varó.

oir, *Berlin Childhood Around 1900*, a task which was made all the more difficult because his collaborator knew no German at all.[15] He also learned of a fund, sponsored by the Rothschilds, that was expressly intended to assist refugee Jewish intellectuals in Paris. But even with this promise of support he still feared that the cost of housing in the city would leave him without sufficient money to cover his everyday expenses.[16] His mood at the time was made even worse by an infection in his thigh; and he reported that a German doctor who was treating him "delights in painting daily pictures of my chances of dying." To Scholem he confided his anxiety about returning to Paris, where nativist groups were now saying "Les émigrés sont pires que les boches" ("The immigrants are worse than the Germans").[17] It was during this time on Ibiza that he composed "Experience and Poverty," in which he offered a grim forecast of the coming years. Technology had destroyed what used to count as authentic experience; the new, highly polished surfaces of modern life were made of glass: they lacked all depth or "aura." It seemed to Benjamin that the only solution might be to embrace this condition without regret, to wipe the slate clean. What was necessary was "a new, positive concept of barbarism," as exemplified by writers and artists such as Bertolt Brecht, Paul Klee, and Paul Scheerbart (the German author of science fiction). Benjamin's tone was ambivalent, split between utopia and despair: "We have given up one portion of the human heritage after another, and have often left it at the pawnbroker's for a hundredth of its true value, in exchange for the small change of 'the contemporary.' The economic crisis is at the door, and behind it is the shadow of the approaching war."[18]

The Alienation Effect

In early October 1933 Benjamin was back in Paris, his financial situation now an urgent concern. The handful of newspapers and journals in which he could still publish his work had dwindled to almost nothing. *Die Literarische Welt* was renamed *Das deutsche Wort*, and swiftly became a tool of Nazi ideology.[19] A similar fate was to befall the *Frankfurter Zeitung*, the left-liberal paper of the Weimar era to which so many intellectuals on the left, both Jewish and non-Jewish, had contributed.[20] Benjamin succeeded in placing two more essays there, but only by adopting the Germanic-sounding pseudonym Detlef Holz.[21] In these uncertain waters the prospect of an affiliation with the Institute for Social Research came as a lifeline. Max Horkheimer, its director, had been among the first members of the faculty to be dismissed from the university in Frankfurt. He now managed it from the branch office in Geneva, before moving the operation to New York the following year. Meanwhile, the Leipzig-based publisher C. L. Hirschfeld informed Horkheimer that he could no longer publish the house journal, the *Zeitschrift für Sozial-*

forschung, which was then transferred to Paris, where its first issue appeared in September.[22] The shift to Paris offered Benjamin a welcome opportunity to strengthen his connections with the Institute for Social Research and its members. Adorno, then living in England (where he was trying without great success to gain the respect of philosophers at Oxford), served as Benjamin's liaison, and an extensive letter from Horkheimer detailed the terms of his affiliation.[23] His first major contribution to the journal was a survey, "On the Contemporary Social Position of the French Writer," which appeared in the spring of 1934. It was the first of his writings for the *Zeitschrift*, many of them on French themes.

Meanwhile, however, Benjamin had deepened his friendship with the leftist poet and playwright Bertolt Brecht, whose politically engagé sensibility and vigorous opinions concerning the proper direction for modern aesthetics was to leave a strong imprint on Benjamin's work. Even before his emigration from Germany, Benjamin had found in Brecht a kindred spirit and source of inspiration. In 1932 he had produced a radio play, "What the Germans Were Reading While Their Classical Authors Were Writing," that was broadcast in Berlin. In a commentary on the radio play, Benjamin explained that the new medium had the potential to transform both aesthetic and political experience. "On the strength of its unprecedented technological potential to address unlimited masses simultaneously, popularization has outgrown its well-meaning, humanistic intentions and [has] become an endeavor with its own formal laws, one that has elevated itself just as markedly from its former practice as did modern advertising technology in the previous century." Radio, he wrote, "demands a total transformation" of cultural material and "mobilizes the public" toward a new species of active knowledge.[24]

Such claims regarding the promise of modern technology—especially the idea that it could stimulate the masses toward a new experience of their own agency—reflected the growing friendship with Brecht, whose influence over Benjamin's work would become more pronounced in the 1930s. They were nevertheless divided by differences in both personal and political temperament. Brecht, a modernist poet and playwright of great originality, was in many respects far more militant. A tough-minded intellectual, he had little patience for his friend's lapses into melancholia and romantic reverie. Brecht was also far less prone to nostalgia. In theatrical works written in collaboration with the composer Kurt Weill, such as "The Threepenny Opera" (1928) and "The Rise and Fall of the City of Mahagonny" (1927–1930), along with theoretical essays such as "The Modern Theatre Is the Epic Theatre" (1930), Brecht sought to shatter the illusions of bourgeois aesthetic experience and expose audiences to the modernist construction of theatrical illusion. By means of this *Verfremdungseffekt*, or "alienation effect," he believed that theater could become a revolutionary force not simply on the level of ideological content but on the level of its form. His hostility to the "culinary" quality of traditional aesthetics went hand in hand with a certain emphasis on thinking in a straightforward manner, or what he called *plumpes Denken*, "blunt thinking" (a phrase he had introduced in his *Threepenny Novel* in 1934).[25]

In early 1933, due to his forthright allegiance to the political left, Brecht and his wife Helene Weigel were compelled to leave Germany. They moved to Denmark, where they acquired a farmhouse in the peaceful island town of Svendborg. Benjamin had been closely involved with Brecht in planning *Krise und Kritik*, a new journal in which they hoped to promote the ideal of an alliance between leftist politics and modernist aesthetics. In a letter to Scholem in 1930 he joked about the composition of the editorial board: "It will give you ambivalent satisfaction," he wrote, "to see my name listed there as the only Jew among all the *goyim*."[26] The following year, Benjamin withdrew from the project, though his friendship with Brecht remained intact. Throughout the 1930s he would visit the Brechts in Denmark, and he even spent long stretches of time at the family home in Svendborg, where he and Brecht often played chess and engaged in debates over art and politics.

Among the more noteworthy signs of their alliance was "The Author as Producer," an address that Benjamin was supposed to deliver in the spring of 1934 at the Institute for the Study of Fascism, a communist group in Paris.[27] In the text of the lecture, Benjamin argues that the old concept of artistic autonomy is now defunct. "The bourgeois writer of entertainment literature," he writes, will refuse to acknowledge the fact that he has allied himself with "certain class interests." However, a new ideal of aesthetics had emerged with Brecht's concept of "epic theater." Its purpose was not "filling the public with feelings, even seditious ones," but rather "alienating it in an enduring way, through thinking, from the conditions in which it lives."[28] This essay, perhaps more than just about any other, speaks to the power of Brecht's influence over Benjamin. To characterize an author as a "producer" is to drive home the Marxist analogy between worker and artist. According to the ideal of aesthetic purity, a poem or a play has no purpose: it is defined simply as *l'art pour l'art,* art for art's sake alone. For Brecht and also for Benjamin, however, this unworldly ideal could no longer be justified: in a society riven by class conflict, art must be enlisted in the struggle for liberation.

In the late summer of 1934, Benjamin vacationed with the Brechts at their Svendborg home, where the warm climate provided a welcome opportunity for bathing and long walks.[29] Despite the everyday pleasures, however, he often fell into a sullen mood, perhaps, as he mused in a letter to Scholem, because his thoughts were preoccupied with the political situation in Germany. It surely did not help matters that he also found himself in a "long, heated debate" with Brecht regarding his essay on Kafka. In notes that he took during his stay in Svendborg, Benjamin recorded Brecht's accusation that the essay promoted "Jewish fascism." Regarding Kafka as a literary talent, Brecht had no generous words. "He was a Jewboy . . . a feeble, unattractive figure, a bubble on the surface of the swamp of Prague's cultural life, and nothing more." Brecht also dismissed Kafka's uncanny story "The Cares of the Family Man" as the transcript of a "homeowner" or "petty bourgeois." This was only one illustration of what Benjamin called "the inflammatory side" of Brecht's thought, which became especially pronounced during a conversation about Dostoyevsky, whose novel *Crime and Punishment* Benjamin was reading at the time. Unlike Benjamin, Brecht openly disdained the works of Dostoyevsky, along with the music of Frédéric Chopin, as mere bits of *Würstchen* (or little sausage).[30] After Benjamin's death, Brecht adopted only a slightly more generous tone in his journal. Regarding the essay "On the Concept of History," Brecht wrote in August 1941 that "the little treatise is clear and presents complex issues simply (despite its metaphors and its Judaisms)."[31]

Such lapses in civility did not deter Benjamin from developing an important friendship with Brecht and even seeking his intellectual guidance. Surely the best-known specimen of this cross-pollination is "The Work of Art in the Age of Its Technical Reproducibility," an essay Benjamin composed with great care and revised extensively between 1935 and 1936. It offers nothing less than a history of aesthetic transformation from art's origins to its most recent possibilities. Art, he claims, was first born as a ritual within the holistic texture of ancient practices of magic. With the rise of religion, the artwork remained a sacred object of veneration, and even when art underwent an apparent secularization of content in the bourgeois era it retained its quasi-religious prestige. The bourgeoisie now gazes upon its artworks in a worshipful posture of concentration and submission. The very ideal of "art for art's sake" is nothing less than a "negative theology" as applied to aesthetics. Traditional art still comes enwreathed in the quasi-sacred quality of uniqueness that Benjamin calls its "aura."

He had used this term before. He explored the concept of the aura at length in 1931, in his essay "Little History of Photography," where he described early daguerreotypes and photographic portraits (such as the portrait of the young Kafka) in which individuals appear as if they are gazing at us from out of the past with "infinite sadness."[32] The nostalgia with which Benjamin describes the aura suggests that he could not report on its disappearance without at least some regret.[33] But he nonetheless sees its disappearance as a crucial step in the emergence of revolutionary aesthetics. With the emergence of modern photography and film, he argues, the aura gradually begins to dissolve. An artwork no longer remains a singular object of veneration that hangs on a wall: with the technologies of reproduction an artwork can shed its uniqueness and circulate freely throughout society. New forms of modernist composition such as montage break the illusion of aesthetic reality and expose the masses to the possibility of non-auratic art. Through modern techniques applied to photography and film, the masses can experience artworks not passively but in a state of distraction. Even their reaction to a popular film by Charlie Chaplin can be progressive, whereas their reaction to a Picasso painting might be "extremely backward." Benjamin concludes with a bold contrast between two modern possibilities. Fascism seeks to wrap the masses once again in the illusion of an aura. Its artistic collaborators (such as the Italian futurist F. T. Marinetti) portray violence itself as if it were an object of beauty, leading to a perverse condition in which the bourgeoisie contemplates its own destruction as if it were an aesthetic event. Fascism thus involves an "aestheticization of politics." Against this possibility Benjamin declares that "Communism responds by politicizing art."[34]

Benjamin had planted the seeds for this argument several years before. In an essay in 1930, "Theories of German Fascism," he accused writers such as Ernst Jünger of an aesthetic of violence.[35] Enchanted with the "cult of war," even after World War I had ended, a new coterie of authors extolled the martial ideal of "total mobilization." They wrote in a delirious, expressionist idiom about the "primeval" and "volcanic" meaning of violence as if it were "the highest revelation of existence." Jünger was a decorated officer who had seen combat in the Battle of the Somme (among other major martial adventures). But he returned from the war less traumatized than enchanted by what he had seen. In works such as *In the Storm of Steel* (*Im Stahlgewitter*), a memoir written in 1920, and *War as Inner Experience* (*Der Kampf als inneres Erlebnis*) from 1922, Jünger refashioned the horrors of wartime violence into a modernist aesthetic in which the stark realities of military service all but vanished into an abstracted poetry of mechanized death. Benjamin dismissed the entirety of this new aesthetic with an angry wave of the hand: it was little more than "sinister runic nonsense." But he also recognized in this idiom the emerging threat of a fascist ideology that, if left unchecked, would turn violence itself into a new mysticism. In a phrase that closely anticipated his later essay on art and technical reproducibility, he defined this fascist aesthetic as "the uninhibited translation of the principles of *l'art pour l'art* to war itself."[36]

This thought-provoking analysis of fascism reflects the obvious influence of Brecht, who discerned in fascism the ultimate expression of a bourgeois preference for illusion over reality. In his plays Brecht sought to shatter the manifold illusions of conventional bourgeois aesthetics by means of an "alienation effect." Much like Brecht, Benjamin had come to believe that modernist aesthetics could fulfill its emancipatory promise only if the artwork were stripped of its aura. Throughout the 1930s he continued to adhere to the Brechtian aesthetic of an artwork without illusion, and he nourished plans for writing a longer monograph on his friend's aesthetic theory. As late as 1939, Benjamin sketched a list, "Material for a discourse on Brecht," in which he named all of the writings he had devoted to Brecht's work.[37] Other friends and colleagues, however, regarded his intellectual and personal proximity to Brecht with great suspicion. Scholem, who found all traces of Marxism in Benjamin's writing distasteful, issued a stern warning., "You are endangered more by your desire for community, even if it be the apocalyptic community of the revolution, than by the horror of loneliness that speaks from so many of your writings."[38]

Adorno, though he did not share Scholem's allergies to Marxism, wrote about Brecht in terms that were no less hostile. In a letter sent to Benjamin from London in 1936, he expressed his forthright concern that the artwork essay reflected the influence of Brecht's "crude thinking." To counter Brecht's ideas, he recommended "*more* dialectics." Specifically, he objected to the view that the ideal of aesthetic autonomy should be wholly condemned as if it were little more than a remnant of bourgeois mystification. "You underestimate the technical character of autonomous art," Adorno wrote, "and overestimate that of dependent art." Most of all, Adorno felt that Benjamin was mistaken to place such unbounded trust in the promises of technical reproducibility, as if the sheer fact of an artwork's circulation in capitalist society would prepare the way for revolution. Technical reproducibility, Adorno warned, had dialectical consequences that could only end in an artwork's destruction. By volatilizing art into a society governed by the exchange principle, the artwork might shed its aura only to be exposed to thoroughgoing commodification. Adorno therefore recommended that Benjamin revise his essay to reflect a more sober assessment of the fate of art in capitalist society. Any traces of Brecht would have to be expunged. The essay could be improved only if Benjamin worked toward "the total elimination of [its] Brechtian motifs." Benjamin would have to reject the Brecht's mythical ideas concerning "the immediacy of aesthetic experience," and he would need to reckon with "the actual consciousness of actual workers." As Adorno explained, workers "enjoy no advantage over their bourgeois counterparts apart from their interest in the revolution, and otherwise [they] bear all the marks of mutilation of the typical bourgeois character."[39] Adorno concluded the letter with a striking phrase: "My own task is to hold your arm steady until the Brechtian sun has finally sunk beneath its exotic waters."[40]

Pearls for Sale

Beginning in the autumn of 1933, Benjamin's connection with the Institute for Social Research grew stronger, and he published several pieces in the *Zeitschrift*, including the artwork essay in a French version. The translation had been prepared by the Parisian novelist and literary critic Pierre Klossowski, who belonged to the circle associated with Georges Bataille and the Collège de Sociologie. Bataille, a highly original philosopher, novelist, and poet who worked at the Bibliothèque Nationale, gave Benjamin a further and much needed entrée into French intellectual circles at a moment when his financial and psychological status had taken a terrific plunge. On December 30, 1933, Benjamin wrote to Gretel Karplus that he was "not only at the end of the old year but also at the end of my wits."[41] He was compelled to continue selling off many of his books, though he was also the beneficiary of funding from the Alliance Israélite Universelle, the Paris-based organization founded in the mid-nineteenth century that had devoted much of its work to defending embattled Jewish communities across the Levant.[42]

To economize further, he relocated from his independent rooms and moved in with his sister Dora in her Parisian flat. Throughout the 1930s, he would also rely on stipends dispensed by the Institute for Social Research. In his correspondence with Horkheimer he declared his intention "to serve the goals of the Institute," and stated his conviction that "collective literary products are particularly suited to materialistic treatment."[43] Further communication with Horkheimer nourished his hopes that he might eventually join the institute in the United States as it began to lay the groundwork for the shift in its offices. Friedrich Pollock, who, alongside Horkheimer, played a major role in the institute's financial matters, assisted Benjamin in securing funds.

The Institute for Social Research did not provide financial assistance only for reasons of charity. As Benjamin's friend, Adorno assumed a special role in helping to convince his colleagues that Benjamin's studies would make a vital contribution to their collective task. In Paris, Benjamin had explained to Pollock the details of his work in progress, "Paris, Capital of the Nineteenth Century," a preparatory sketch for *The Arcades Project.* Adorno in particular felt that the project held great promise, and to his colleagues he wrote that it had stood "at the center of my discussions with Benjamin over the last ten years." In a June 1935 letter to Horkheimer he offered further praise. "I regard this piece as Benjamin's *chef d'oeuvre,* something which will prove to be of the greatest imaginable theoretical significance, and indeed . . . if such a word is appropriate for us here . . . brilliant in conception."[44] The stipends, though modest in sum, provided the encouragement and material support Benjamin desperately needed. To Adorno he wrote in gratitude, "My work on the Arcades has begun to revive and it is you yourself who have breathed life into the embers." He spent most of his daytime hours in the reading room of the Bibliothèque Nationale, where he had "even come to feel quite at home with the rather officious *règlement* of the place." His habitat, with its vaulted, light-filled ceiling and the painted trees that adorned the walls, was "one of the most remarkable reading rooms in the world." While seated there at his desk he felt as if he were "surrounded by an operatic set."[45]

The Arcades Project, or *Passagenwerk*, surely ranks among the unique works of the twentieth century, even though its author left it unfinished. As early as 1923 Benjamin had begun to translate and write commentaries on Charles Baudelaire, whose poetry and prose became the key point of entry for diving into the cultural history of nineteenth-century Paris. By the later 1920s the project had greatly expanded in scope: Benjamin had read *Le paysan de Paris*, the surrealist novel published in 1926 by Louis Aragon: "Evenings, lying in bed, I could never read more than two to three pages by him because my heart started to pound so hard that I had to put the book down!"[46] The cause of his excitement was the novel's portrait of *passages*, the glass-roofed corridors lined on either side with elegant shops in whose vitrines the Parisian bourgeoisie could gaze upon all of the items for sale. The gray-green light that filtered down into the arcades gave the impression of a sunken cathedral or an Atlantis, as if one were strolling through a department store undersea. Also hidden within the arcades were dioramas, dark theaters that displayed all of the exotic corners of the globe. In one lyrical note for his project, Benjamin sought to convey the strangeness of the atmosphere:

> The innermost glowing cells of the city of light, the old dioramas, nested in the arcades, one of which still bears the name [Passage des Panoramas]. *It was, at first glance, as though one had stepped into an aquarium.* Along the wall of the great darkened hall, broken at intervals by narrow joints, it stretched like a ribbon of illuminated water behind glass [*wie ein Band hinter Glas erleuchteten Wassers entlang*]. The play of colors among deep-sea fauna cannot burn more powerfully.[47]

This was only one sample of the insights that Benjamin recorded in his notes. Over many years he assembled a massive collection of quotations, observations, historical facts, and personal comments, each of which was plucked from his reading like a pearl from the ocean floor. In a photograph taken by the avant-garde photographer Germaine Krull in 1929, one can see the Passage du Caire in the 2nd arrondissement, the very oldest of all the Parisian passages. Halfway down the arcade there hangs a sign for a shop that specialized in pearls (*Perles*).

As he deepened his interest in Marx's analysis of capitalism, Benjamin came to see the arcade as a "dialectical image" that condensed into one vision the entire dreamscape of the commodified world. The name of Karl Marx, however, makes a rather belated appearance in his work. Although Benjamin had read other Marxist theorists in the 1920s (including such milestones of philosophical Marxism as Lukács's *History and Class Consciousness*), he was inclined, by both intellect and personal temperament, to eclecticism in his reading. Anarchistic in spirit, he was not predisposed to thinking within a single theoretical system, no matter how capacious its claims. His proximity to both Lacis and Brecht no doubt stimulated his further interest in Marxism, but it was most of all his affiliation with the Institute for Social Research in the thirties that pushed him toward reconceiving the *Arcades Project* as a contribution to the Marxist theory of bourgeois culture.

Only in June 1935 could he report to Adorno in a letter that he had begun to explore the "mighty Alpine heights" of Marx's work represented by the first volume of *Capital*.[48] Later that same year he met with Friedrich Pollock in Paris, and he was encouraged to write out a précis for the entire project. Submitted to the institute with the title "Paris, the Capital of the Nineteenth Century," the précis was supposed to demonstrate that he was working toward what he now called "a materialist theory of art."[49] His study would explore every facet of nineteenth-century Paris—from the arcades to the panoramas, and from the origins of photography to the world exhibition of 1867, not to mention the poetry of Baudelaire (with its portraits of flâneurs, ragpickers, drunkards, and prostitutes) and the dramatic transformation of the city's topography under the direction of

Passage du Caire, Paris, circa 1928 (Photograph by Germaine Krull; copyright, Estate Germaine Krull, Museum Folkwang, Essen)

Baron Haussmann. Benjamin wished to show that in the nineteenth century "the monuments of the bourgeoisie" appear as *ruins* "even before they have crumbled." The result would be a genuinely dialectical study: it would reveal the urban environment as both a "dream world" and a place of "awakening."[50]

It is one of the great tragedies of the *Arcades Project*, however, that Benjamin could not pursue his own most creative insights without disappointing at least one faction of his readers. The harder he tried to satisfy his colleagues at the institute by demonstrating his Marxist theoretical credentials, the less satisfied they seemed with the results. The crucial period of transition, bringing to an end his "rhapsodic naïveté" and his turn to Marxism, came about in conversations with many colleagues and friends: Adorno, Lacis, Horkheimer, and Gretel Karplus (whom he affectionately called "Felizitas"), and then with Brecht, all of whom helped him to recast the project in terms that might appear more consonant with historical materialism. In the early summer of 1935, Adorno and Horkheimer received the précis, and Benjamin awaited their verdict. In August there came at last a response from Adorno, who was then staying briefly in the town of Hornberg in the Black Forest. His letter was unusually long and detailed.

The response was not at all what Benjamin might have hoped. Adorno fastened upon the phrase "Chaque époque rêve la suivante" ("Every epoch dreams the one that follows"). With this methodological principle, Benjamin had meant to encapsulate his idea of a "dialectical image." No historical age is wholly self-enclosed: even its smallest and most insignificant artifacts contain within themselves the explosive energy that may eventually lead to the undoing of the age. Adorno urged Benjamin to clarify this point. Although he was by no means opposed to this idea in principle, Adorno expressed his concern that in its present form the essay was insufficiently dialectical: It seemed to suggest that the dreams were contents of collective consciousness, an implication with dangerously Jungian and psychologistic undertones. The idea of a dialectical image thereby lost its materialist status and its "objective" promise of freedom. "The fetish character of the commodity is not a fact of consciousness," Adorno explained, "it is dialectical in the preeminent sense of producing consciousness." Adorno concluded the Hornberg letter with an excuse for "the carping nature" of his comments, but the half-hearted apology did little to diminish its injurious effect.[51] Benjamin plunged into a new phase of depression.

All the same, Benjamin tried his best to take the criticism seriously. From that point onward, the *Arcades Project* underwent a considerable shift, away from the language of dreams and psychology and toward an interpretation that assumed (at least in appearance) the guise of a more objective and materialist understanding of culture.[52] Horkheimer and others at the institute were keen to see the fruits of his efforts. In 1938 Benjamin drafted plans for a less sprawling work, tentatively titled "The Paris of the Second Empire in Baudelaire," that would fasten upon Baudelaire's poetry and its relation to the French capital. He submitted an extended portion of the book for publication to the Institute for Social Research, which by this point had relocated to Morningside Heights, just around the corner from Columbia University on New York's Upper West Side.

The surviving text of the Paris essay exemplifies Benjamin's interpretive acumen at its finest. Baudelaire's portrait gallery of modern life as captured in such poems as "Le Vin des chiffoniers" ("The Ragpickers' Wine") became allegories of social precarity with a potential for social upheaval. Marx himself had once described the threadbare counterculture of *la bohême*, another segment of the dangerous classes, as "indeterminate, disintegrated, fluctuating mass," out of which there might arise the threat of proletarian conspiracy.[53] Baudelaire himself, though he is a man of letters, knows that his profession is like that of a prostitute. In a poem omitted from *Les fleurs du mal* he writes:

In order to have shoes, she has sold her soul;
But the good Lord would laugh if, beside this reviled woman,
I aped Tartuffe and put on airs,
I, who sell my thoughts, and would be an author.[54]

Not unlike the *Berlin Chronicle* and *One-Way Street*, the Paris essay is an exercise in urban poetics. It ventures out of the arcades and onto the streets, but then steps into the department store, a "labyrinth of commodities" in which the flâneur-as-poet makes his last promenade and becomes a commodity himself.[55] Benjamin describes Baudelaire as an artist who is embittered by penury and constantly on the alert for a possible sale: "he goes to the marketplace as a flâneur—ostensibly to look around, but in truth to find a buyer." In writing such a phrase, Benjamin no doubt recognized himself. Although one should not conflate literary analysis with biography, certain passages in the Paris essay leave the reader uncertain whether Benjamin meant to summarize a poem by Baudelaire or wished only to describe his own condition.

The autobiographical aspect of the essay becomes even more evident when Benjamin fastens his eye on passages in which Baudelaire offers a portrait of the *chiffonnier*, or ragpicker. Baudelaire draws an analogy between the ragpicker and the poet:

> Here we have a man whose job it is to gather the day's refuse in the capital. Everything that the big city has thrown away, everything it has lost, everything it has scorned, everything it has crushed underfoot he catalogues and collects. He collates the annals of intemperance, the capharnaum of waste. He sorts things out and selects judiciously; he collects, like a miser guarding a treasure, refuse which will assume the shape of useful or gratifying objects between the jaws of the goddess of Industry.[56]

About this passage Benjamin offers an insightful remark:

> The description is one extended metaphor for the poetic method, as Baudelaire practiced it. Ragpicker and poet: both

> are concerned with refuse, and both go about their solitary business while other citizens are sleeping. . . . This is the gait of the poet who roams the city in search of rhyme-booty; it is also the gait of the ragpicker, who is obliged to come to a halt every few moments to gather up the refuse he encounters.[57]

Benjamin surely knew that he was not only pursuing an analysis of Baudelaire. He was also painting a self-portrait, and a record of his own daily labors in the Bibliothèque Nationale. When he wrote of Baudelaire he might have been describing himself: "Flâneur, apache, dandy, and ragpicker were so many roles to him. For the modern hero is no hero; he is a portrayer of heroes. Heroic modernity turns out to be a *Trauerspiel* in which the hero's part is available." Picking through the ruins of the city like a baroque prince, Benjamin resembled Baudelaire, "on the lookout for banal incidents in order to liken them to poetic events."[58]

On November 10, 1938, Benjamin received word from the institute that it did not intend to publish the essay. Adorno was tasked with writing the letter of rejection, but it conveyed a judgment that was shared in common by Max Horkheimer and Leo Löwenthal as well. In their collective opinion, the essay did not live up to the principles of dialectical materialism, since it lacked the key element of mediation. It presented objective matters such as a wine tax in direct relation to cultural phenomena such as Baudelaire's poem "L'âme du vin," as if the connection between them were causal. This resulted in what Adorno called an "immediate" materialism in which Benjamin had "abruptly and crudely" joined together "the Baudelairean world of forms" with "the harsh necessities of life." A more sophisticated version of historical materialism would need to forgo the simplistic and unidirectional model of culture as a mere precipitate of the economic base.

Adorno recognized that the essay exemplified its author's

skill for fixing upon the most minute details, even to the point of celebrating the nominalist idea that each item in the world possesses its irreplaceable name. The idea, theological in origin, had undeniable merit, but even this skill could be abused. Adorno had quarreled with Benjamin over matters before, and he did not mince words now. "To express the matter another way: the theological motif of calling things by their names tends to switch into the wide-eyed presentation of mere facts. If one wanted to put it rather drastically, one could say that your study is located at the crossroads of magic and positivism."[59]

The accusation was brutal. Benjamin prided himself on his interpretive skills, but Adorno seemed to imply that the essay had abandoned the work of interpretation altogether. The institute's verdict on the Paris essay was (in the words of Michael Jennings) "arguably the most crushing rejection of [Benjamin's] career."[60] Whether the critical judgment of the essay was at all fair is a different question entirely. But it surely did not help that in the very same letter Adorno mentioned the forthcoming publication of his own essay, "The Fetish Character in Music," in which he touched upon their long-running disagreement over the fate of art in a commodified world.[61] Although Adorno made no explicit mention of Benjamin in the essay, the implied criticism was obvious: by celebrating the reproducibility of modern art Benjamin had neglected the baleful effects of capitalist exchange. In the acid bath of commodification true art could not survive; it simply withered.

Benjamin received the letter of rejection at an especially bad time, both personally and financially. Between 1934 and 1938 Benjamin moved in and out of different flats in Paris and made frequent trips abroad, to stay with the Brechts but also to San Remo, where Dora Kellner was living with Stefan while managing the Villa Verde. Benjamin's arrival in San Remo in the winter of 1934 raised his hopes; he had not seen his son in two years and there were plans that Stefan might transfer to a local school.[62] Although he had intended to stay for much longer, he was compelled to leave San Remo early due to the arrival of Dora's mother. At this time he also received word from Paris that his sister Dora had fallen ill.[63] Upon his return he lived briefly in a hotel and then, through the summer of 1935 while Dora was away, he stayed briefly at her flat. He then shifted to a sublet in the rue Bérnard in the 14th arrondissement, where he was able to remain for nearly two years.

Meanwhile the political situation in France had grown far worse. In the climate of rising xenophobia, Jews, and especially Jewish immigrants, found themselves increasingly vulnerable. In the first year following the Nazi seizure of power an estimated 25,000 Germans moved to France, of which 85 percent were Jews.[64] Though at first they were welcomed by the government, the change to a more conservative regime, under Pierre-Étienne Flandin and Pierre Laval, meant a restoration of more restrictive asylum policies, motivated in part by concerns for competition over employment during the economic disarray of the Depression. In 1936 the formation of the Popular Front under the leadership of the socialist Léon Blum, an Alsatian Jew, had the effect of further exacerbating popular anti-Semitism, even while it also intensified the demand for governmental measures to stop the influx of immigrants. Following Nazi Germany's *Anschluss* in March 1938, the number of Austrian-Jewish refugees in France began to swell to record heights, and the French government passed new laws to block their arrival.[65]

The reception of Jewish refugees beyond the European continent was hardly more favorable. Despite efforts by President Franklin D. Roosevelt, the refugee crisis in the United States persisted due to a quota system, and even after September 1938 the waiting period for a visa to America grew to a minimum of nine years.[66] In Germany, the massive wave of riots and assaults on Jews, Jewish businesses, and synagogues known as *Kristall-*

nacht (November 9–10, 1938) resulted in the arrest of about 30,000 Jews who were sent to concentration camps, but the flow of refugees did not result in a change of the official U.S. quotas. Meanwhile, in Palestine, hostility among the Arab population toward the Jews was growing stronger. In June 1936, Scholem wrote to Benjamin, "The Arabs have been waging genuine partisan warfare over the last four weeks, with an intensity that keeps escalating and exhibits an unexpected terror and barbarism."[67] Due to the violence of the riots a curfew was declared in Jerusalem, and Scholem remarked on the sound of "incessant shooting" that came from the surrounding hills. Later that month Benjamin responded with a letter of sympathy from Paris, expressing his fear that "the psychological reactions of the Jews might prove scarcely less harmful than the physical actions of the Arabs." Scholem, though ardent in his commitment to Zionism, had long advocated peaceful coexistence and restraint. He had been among the early members of Brit Shalom, the group founded in 1925 that supported the ideal of a binational state. Many prominent figures joined the group or declared their support, including Martin Buber, Judah Magnes, and Albert Einstein. In its founding charter (made public in 1927) it called for the creation of "a common life between Hebrews and Arabs in the Land of Israel on the foundation of fully equal political rights for the two nations with broad autonomy [for each]."[68]

In the mid-1930s, however, growing hostility between the two populations made even this binational ideal appear increasingly remote. In a letter Scholem reported in August 1936 that Levi Billig, an assistant professor of Arab literature, had been killed "while reading a book in his study."[69] But Scholem was even less hopeful about the chances for Jewish life elsewhere. Scholem's own brother Werner, a communist (and therefore less disposed to move to Palestine), had been in prison since 1933, until 1938 when he was deported to Buchenwald. In 1940 he was executed. Benjamin's brother Georg was also arrested for his communist activities; he was later imprisoned in the Mauthausen concentration camp, where he was killed in 1942. Already in 1936, Benjamin wrote to Scholem that he did not see the situation in Europe as any more promising than the situation in Palestine.[70] Everywhere one looked, it seemed, Jews were unwelcome.

Knowing that actual emigration to Palestine was unlikely, Benjamin began as early as May 1936 to seek a means to secure French citizenship. But he encountered many delays, not least due to rising antipathy in France against Jewish refugees from Germany.[71] In the spring of 1937, Scholem wrote with an invitation, suggesting that Benjamin come stay with him and his (second) wife Fania that coming winter in their Jerusalem home. Regarding the political situation, Scholem noted that he was "personally against partition" and still felt that "joint Arab-Jewish sovereignty in the whole of Palestine" would prove the ideal solution, though he admitted that it was a solution that "will probably never be granted." Benjamin responded favorably to this invitation, writing that he would be pleased to make the visit. Over the next month, however, the plan for a trip to Palestine once again disintegrated, chiefly because Benjamin found the cost of the trip prohibitive, but also because he knew that his German passport would soon be invalid and the prospect of travel without official papers was unimaginable.[72] Meanwhile, his living situation in Paris had only grown worse. He was unable to move back into his previous lodgings as he had hoped, and his new quarters, though rent-free, were (in his words) "wretched." The flat was located on the ground floor on a major thoroughfare outside the Parisian periphery, where Benjamin could hear the roar of "countless trucks" as they rolled by "from morning to night."[73]

In spring 1938, Friedrich Pollock passed through Paris, and Benjamin had the chance to meet with him in person to discuss his affiliation and convey the difficulties of his current situation. Among other topics they discussed the urgent question of French naturalization or emigration to the United States. "The formal process involved here," he explained to Adorno, "is incredibly tedious."[74] The French application required that he assemble a dossier with letters of support, which he was able to secure from luminaries such as André Gide and Paul Valéry. Complications ensued chiefly because of his frequent shifts of domicile, but an official informed him that, if he lacked proof of residency, he could submit a work certificate instead. Accordingly, Benjamin asked that Horkheimer provide him with a letter to verify that since the summer of 1934 he had been working for the Institute for Social Research in Paris. Although he felt some optimism about the success of his application, he had come to understand that the prefecture in Paris was currently examining 90,000 separate dossiers. In a letter to Horkheimer in May 1939 he wrote that "naturalizations at the moment are non-existent." By this point his greatest wish was to make his way to the United States.[75]

Last Years in Paris

During his final years in Paris, Benjamin continued to receive financial support from the institute. He contributed several essays to the *Zeitschrift*, including the intellectual portrait of Eduard Fuchs (1870–1940), the cultural historian whose work, especially his fascination for collecting, furnished a model for Benjamin's theory of historical materialism. Fuchs was a notorious *ramasseur*, or packrat, about whom it was said, "C'est le monsieur qui mange tout Paris" ("This is the gentleman who consumes all of Paris").[76] Fuchs was both celebrated and condemned for his three-volume history of erotic art, and his illustrated history of manners from the Middle Ages to the present. He also served as an inspiration for Benjamin's own cultural-historical efforts in the *Passagenwerk*. Benjamin writes of Fuchs:

> The alchemist, in his "base" desire to make gold, carries out research on the chemicals in which planets and elements come together in images of spiritual man; by the same token, in satisfying the "base" desire for possession, this collector carries out research on an art in whose creatives the productive forces and the masses come together in images of historical man.[77]

Benjamin found in Fuchs a kindred spirit, a collector who embraced "anonymous artists" far more than venerated masters. His ecumenical approach to "mass art" contributed more to "the humanization of mankind" than any "cult of the leader," which, Benjamin warned, was once again descending upon civilization. In this essay Benjamin displays perhaps more strongly than anywhere else his constant oscillation between enthusiasm and melancholy. It was in this essay that he first formulated the well-known dictum: "There is no document of culture which is not at the same time a document of barbarism."[78]

Between April 1938 and February 1939 he also wrote "Central Park," notes chiefly consisting in a discussion of Baudelaire. But these notes also reflect a darkening of the political horizon. Benjamin clearly sensed the coming cataclysm:

> To interrupt the course of the world—that was Baudelaire's deepest intention. The intention of Joshua. Not so much the prophetic one, for he gave no thought to any sort of reform. From this intention sprang his violence, his impatience, and his anger; from it, too, sprang the ever-renewed attempts to stab the world in the heart or sing it to sleep.[79]

Perhaps more succinctly than ever before, Benjamin articulates, with Baudelaire as his muse, the bold claim that one must *interrupt* the historical continuum instead of hoping for immanent signs of progress. "Salvation [*Rettung*] depends on the tiny break [*Sprung*] in the continuous catastrophe."[80] This idea—that redemption demands not progress *through* history but a break with history's normal course—was to become the pivotal theme in one of his very last essays on the concept of history.

After he had received the news from Adorno that the *Zeitschrift* would not publish "Paris of the Second Empire in Baudelaire," Benjamin and Adorno engaged in an extensive correspondence. Their deliberations resulted in a commission for a new essay, "On Some Motifs in Baudelaire." Composed in the early months of 1939, Benjamin completed it and sent it off to Horkheimer on August 1, accompanied by an explanatory note in which he laid out the full details of his intentions.[81] The new essay still addressed various themes in Baudelaire's poetry, though with far less attention to historical and material detail. It portrays Baudelaire as a theorist of urban life:

> L'homme y passe à travers des forêts de symboles
> Qui l'observent avec des regards familiers.
>
> [Man wends his way through forests of symbols,
> Which look at him with their familiar glances.][82]

According to Benjamin, Baudelaire's poems are transcripts of *experience* (*Erfahrung*). This term comes freighted with great significance, not least because it was the topic of his very first essay, published pseudonymously in 1913.[83] Unlike the isolation of "lived" experience (*Erlebnis*) as valorized by traditionalist thinkers such as Wilhelm Dilthey or proto-fascist thinkers such as Ludwig Klages and C. G. Jung, Baudelaire recognizes in modernity "the alienating, blinding experience" of the industrial age. In his poetry he transcribes "the increasing atrophy of experience" as the urban crowd is exposed to the shock of incessant stimuli: he places "shock-experience" (*Chockerfahrung*) at "the very center of his art."[84] Any such shock contributes to "the disintegration of the aura." Benjamin concludes the essay with a striking quotation from Baudelaire's diaries:

> Perdu dans ce villain monde, *coudoyé par les foules*, je suis comme un homme lassé dont l'oeil ne voit en arrière, dans les années profonds, que désabusement et amertume, et devant lui, qu'un orage où rien de neuf n'est contenu, ni enseignement ni douleur.
>
> [Lost in this base world, jostled by the crowd, I am like a weary man whose eye, looking backward into the depths of the years, sees only disillusion and bitterness, and looking ahead sees only a storm which contains nothing new, neither instruction nor pain.][85]

In this essay Baudelaire is transformed from a poet into a historian: he is caught between past and future but finds no consolation in either direction. If he gazes backward he does so without regret, and if he gazes forward he discovers little that would encourage him as a sign of progress—there is only a "storm." In the poet's self-portrait, we can already discern the faint outlines of another figure whom Benjamin would later call "the angel of history." Once he had sent the Baudelaire study off to Horkheimer, Benjamin wrote to Adorno to express his hopes that the essay would appear as planned in the journal's next issue. He concluded with an enigmatic sentence: "I will let my Christian Baudelaire be taken into heaven by nothing but Jewish angels."[86]

Through the late spring and summer of 1939 his letters to the institute grew increasingly urgent in tone. He was still awaiting news regarding his application for French citizenship, but the situation seemed unlikely to be resolved any time soon. Rumors of an imminent war were now widespread, and Benjamin pressed both Horkheimer and Pollock for further information regarding the prospects for his coming to the States. He planned to make inquiries with the American consulate in

Paris concerning a visitor's visa, and he expressed his great fear of what might happen should he be stranded during wartime in France, where foreign residents could face the possibility of internment in a concentration camp.[87] Knowing very well that the financial costs of emigration would be high, he considered what personal possessions he might sell, including more portions of his cherished library. He also made inquiries with an old acquaintance from Berlin, Stephan Lackner (born Morgenroth), an art dealer and writer who had emigrated to New York, to learn if it might be possible to sell his beloved *Angelus Novus*.[88] Since its purchase nearly two decades before, Klee's angel had been among Benjamin's most faithful companions. Letting it go would be like saying farewell to an alter ego.

By this point many of his old acquaintances had departed, and he found himself in a state of painful isolation. Most of the institute's members had departed for the States, the Scholems were in Palestine, the Brechts had left their home in Denmark for Stockholm, though they, too, would soon move to America. The previous autumn, anti-Semitic legislation had taken effect in Italy; Dora Kellner and their son Stefan had moved to England, and she tried to persuade Benjamin to follow, but without success.[89] In April and May 1939 he was the beneficiary of a grant for study for several weeks at the Foyer International d'Étude et Repos, an academic institution housed in a restored abbey in Potigny, a town in northwestern France. Although the private rooms were outfitted with "monastic severity," Benjamin found the premises uncongenial for work due to the noise from other guests. In late May he returned to Paris, only to receive terrible news. The German embassy conveyed the decree that Benjamin had been officially stripped of his German citizenship. Stranded in Paris, he now found himself a stateless Jew, the legal equivalent of a soul in purgatory.[90]

EPILOGUE

The Flight South

Throughout the summer of 1939, Benjamin was preoccupied with completing "On Some Motifs in Baudelaire." He wrote at a furious pace in response to Horkheimer's promise that it could be published in the *Zeitschrift* if it were delivered without delay. The summer's end, however, brought the opening phase of the war. On August 23, Hitler and Stalin signed the non-aggression pact; on September 1, German troops invaded Poland on multiple fronts and converged on Warsaw. On September 3, the British and the French responded by declaring war on Germany; the USSR, now in alliance with the Third Reich, invaded Poland from the east, and Poland was split in two. Benjamin did not require further proof that Paris was also in imminent danger of invasion. He fled the city and sought refuge in Chauconin, a town just to the east where he could stay at least for a short while with Lou Betz (the wife of Maurice Betz, a translator of works by Rilke and Thomas Mann).

In early September Benjamin wrote a brief note to Horkheimer "for no reason than to give you a sign of life."[1] In a postscript he requested a copy of "The Jews and Europe," an essay Horkheimer had just composed for the latest volume of the institute's journal, now published in English in the United States.[2] There is strong evidence that Benjamin read the essay, which appeared in a volume of the journal that also contained an essay of his own. It is doubtful, however, that it would have given Benjamin anything more than cold comfort, since it conveyed little awareness of the specific difficulties European Jews were facing at the time. The essay framed the problem of anti-Semitism in rather simplistic Marxist terms as if it were a crisis of capitalism, and it offered an apocalyptic forecast: "Anti-Semitism will come to a natural end in the totalitarian order when nothing humane remains, although a few Jews might." But Horkheimer also permitted himself some philosophical remarks in praise of Judaism:

> The Jews were once proud of abstract monotheism, their rejection of idolatry, their refusal to make something finite an absolute. Their distress today points them back. Disrespect for anything mortal that puffs itself up as a god is the religion of those who cannot resist devoting their life to the preparation of something better, even in the Europe of the Iron Heel.[3]

Despite these bracing words, the essay as a whole seemed to imply that anti-Semitism served merely as a "safety valve" and belonged to fascism only in its "ascendent phase." Horkheimer did not realize (and neither, to be charitable, did many others realize in 1939) that eliminationist anti-Semitism was an essential and ineradicable feature of the movement's ethno-racial vision. Benjamin asked Scholem for his opinion of the essay, and in response Scholem expressed his outrage without restraint: it was an "entirely useless product" that merely repeated the "cliché" regarding Jews as "agents of circulation," and offered no insights whatsoever into the actual condition of the "unallegorizable Jew and *his* concerns within mankind."[4]

This was to be the last direct exchange between Benjamin and his friend Scholem. Shortly after writing Horkheimer from Chauconin, Benjamin learned of the new governmental decree: as an immigrant from an enemy country who lacked papers of French naturalization, he was obliged to present himself at the Stade de Colombes just outside Paris. From there he was transported to an internment camp in the Château de Vernuche in Nevers, a journey of about two hours by train. Once he had arrived in Nevers he sent a letter to Adrienne Monnier, a writer and publisher who, in 1915, had opened La Maison des Amis des Livres, one of the famed bookstores in Paris that was frequented by the literary avant-garde.[5] Men in physically acceptable condition sought to escape internment by presenting themselves for military service. Benjamin said that he, too, would have liked "absolutely to serve our cause with all of my powers," though his physical condition unfortunately made this impossible. The poet and novelist Hans Sahl, a German Jew who was interned together with Benjamin, later recalled that his companion found the march from the train station to the château exceptionally difficult; a younger man had assisted him by carrying his suitcase. When they arrived, the camp doctors insisted that Benjamin remain at rest. In his memoir Sahl describes the conditions they found when they reached the completely empty château: "there was absolutely nothing, no furniture, no tables, no chairs, not even a single nail from which one could hang one's belongings. We threw ourselves in exhaustion on the naked, polished parquet floor and immediately fell asleep."[6]

Benjamin was confined to the internment camp at Nevers for approximately two months. His physical condition was by his own estimation "mediocre," the rainy conditions did not help to improve matters, and there was little he could do to keep himself busy.[7] As often as possible he wrote letters to friends and colleagues, asking for their assistance in securing his release. To Sylvia Beach (the famed founder of Shakespeare and Company who was also on friendly terms with Monnier) he wrote a brief and exceedingly polite letter simply to request "a bar of chocolate or some cigarettes."[8] Hans Sahl offered a detailed portrait of life in the camp, and remarked on the "rather ironic" fact that "the organizational genius of the prisoners, who never ceased being German during their incarceration, won out over the French disorganization."

> "German" hard work, "German" order, cleanliness, and a sense for discipline and obedience took control of the camp inmates, otherwise hampered by their Jewish self-reflection. A *Wandervogel* spirit behind barbed wire swept rooms with straw brooms, hung wash out to dry, organized lectures comparing Jung, Lenin, and Trotsky. A community that began to function was soon fashioned from the void; from chaos and helplessness emerged a society.[9]

Benjamin himself assumed the tasks that were most suitable to his skills. He held a course outdoors "for advanced students," and he charged a fee of "three Gauloises [cigarettes] or a button." Remarkably, despite the harsh circumstances, he even hatched the idea that he might found a literary journal, but, not unlike the University of Muri, it never got beyond the early stages of planning. One evening Sahl and Benjamin stood at the barbed wire fence and observed the sheep that were grazing in peace on the other side, wholly oblivious to the world at war. "Just to sit once more on the terrace of a café and twiddle my thumbs," Benjamin mused, "that's all I wish for."[10]

In mid-November 1939, Benjamin was finally released, thanks to the combined effort of several acquaintances. He sent a special letter of gratitude to Monnier, who had also enlisted the support of PEN, the international writers' organization. In a letter to Scholem he noted that he had been among the very first to regain his freedom. Although he had lost weight he was otherwise in good condition.[11] In a letter to Horkheimer, he reported that he had returned to his flat on the rue Dombasle. He was also pleased to discover that the Bibliothèque Nationale had been reopened, and it was his greatest wish to renew his studies there as soon as possible. Meanwhile he devoted his energies to planning for his emigration to the United States, and he sought to work out the details with the institute.[12] All hope now seemed to lie in the prospect of a new life in America.

On November 17, he received notice that an application for an American visa had been submitted to the Paris branch of the National Refugee Service, with the assistance of Cecilia Razovsky, a social worker in the Paris office who had earlier worked for the National Council of Jewish Women.[13] Benjamin was grateful for the news but knew very well that he would also require an exit visa from France.[14] Meanwhile he began to look for a professor who could help him in learning English, though he boasted to Gretel Adorno that even without formal lessons he could read the English-language letters that she sent from New York without difficulty.[15] Notwithstanding these efforts, however, the prospect of leaving Paris left him with feelings of great ambivalence. Like his distant relative Heinrich Heine, he had found in France not just a place of refuge but a *Wahlheimat*, an adopted home.[16]

In mid-December he wrote to Horkheimer: "I don't need to tell you how much I feel myself attached to France, by my ties here and by my studies. Nothing in the world, for me, could replace the Bibliothèque Nationale. Moreover, I can only cherish the welcome that I have found in France since [1933]; the benevolence of the authorities and the devotion of my friends."[17] Horkheimer sought to assure him that the institute would extend him the same financial support whether he came to the United States or stayed in France. "You are part of the little group of our members upon whom our theoretical work entirely depends."[18] Such reassurances naturally gave him grounds for hope, even if the technical matters of emigration remained unsettled.[19] At least for the short term he remained in Paris. On January 11 he was able to renew his reader's card for the Bibliothèque Nationale and he resumed his usual habits, diving into his research like the otter into the depths of his cistern. He loved to hide.

Uncertain Messiah

Around February 1940, Benjamin announced in a letter to Horkheimer that he had commenced writing something new: "a certain number of theses on the concept of history."[20] Composed as a series of aphorisms and illustrated with unusual metaphors, the "theses" condense into only a few pages an original conception of historical materialism. All the more surprising, however, are the theological images with which Benjamin seeks to elucidate his claims. The theses open with the image of a chess-playing puppet who seems to be a mere automaton but has the seemingly miraculous ability to defeat all opponents. Hidden beneath the chessboard is a "hunchbacked dwarf" who manipulates the puppet's movements. Benjamin proposes that this puppet can be understood as an illustration of "historical materialism." It can win every game but only if it "enlists the services of theology, which today, as we know, is small and ugly and has to keep out of sight."[21]

This allegory, or "dialectical image," leaves itself open to multiple interpretations. It is quite possibly an homage to Brecht, with whom Benjamin had so often played actual games of chess during his stays in Denmark.[22] But the image serves only as the starting point for Benjamin's highly original reflections on the relationship between historical materialism and theology. All forms of socialist revisionism (such as the one promoted by Eduard Bernstein) rely on a model of history as an unbroken path of progress: the technological mastery of nature is supposed to guarantee a gradual increase in human powers that will result, as if by evolution alone, in the achievement of freedom. The very same model of history also underwrites the methods and philosophies of nineteenth-century historicism, all of which see the historical continuum as a linear arc in which those who emerge as the political victors receive the greatest empathy. Benjamin wishes to break with this model of history. Historical materialism, he insists, must adopt an entirely different idea of time. History should not be understood as a homogenous continuum; rather it must be conceived as if broken into discontinuous moments each of which holds the potential for redemption. Benjamin does not mean to imply that historical materialism itself is nothing but a covert theology. His point is more subtle: historical materialism owes its explanatory strength to concepts that have their origin in theology. In one of his notes for the theses, Benjamin explains: "In the idea of classless society, Marx secularized the idea of messianic time."[23] Although historical materialism cannot be understood as an explicitly messianic doctrine, it nonetheless carries "a *weak* messianic power."[24]

To illustrate this extraordinary claim Benjamin describes his beloved painting by Klee, the *Angelus Novus.* He now calls it "the angel of history." The angel turns his face toward the past. While humanity sees "a chain of events," the angel sees "one single catastrophe, which keeps piling wreckage upon wreckage and hurls it at his feet." The angel is not an agent of redemption but merely its witness. Undeceived by myths of progress, it discerns with open eyes what history actually is:

> The angel would like to stay, awaken the dead, and make whole what has been smashed. But a storm is blowing from Paradise and has got caught in his wings; it is so strong that the angel can no longer close them. This storm drives him irresistibly into the future, to which his back is turned, while

> the pile of debris before him grows toward the sky. What we call progress is *this* storm.[25]

With this image Benjamin means to convey the thought that history resembles a ruin, a theatrical stage upon which humanity enacts its endless *Trauerspiel.* Like the baroque dramas to which Benjamin had devoted his unsuccessful bid for habilitation, history is revealed as a drama without meaning or direction. Full of "sound and fury," it signifies nothing.

The political implications of Benjamin's image are uncertain. If historical events amount to little more than a pile of debris, then it is unclear why human effort should be directed toward one particular end over another. The very idea of progress becomes the ultimate palliative, little more than a bourgeois fantasy. In this idea we can still discern the influence of Carl Schmitt, who looked to theology for a higher sense of political purpose. But Benjamin has reversed Schmitt's authoritarian lesson. For Benjamin, unlike Schmitt, the "state of emergency" in which we live is "not the exception but the rule."[26] Like Schmitt, however, Benjamin seems to hold fast to the promise of a theological solution. The angel wishes to "make whole" what has been shattered, an image that bears an unmistakable resemblance to the idea of *tikkun ha-olam*, or the repair of the world. This was a theme from the Lurianic Kabbalah that Benjamin would have learned from Scholem. Unlike Scholem, however, Benjamin means to enlist this theme for a purely secular and political cause. Fascism can be defeated, he argues, only if we abandon the illusory idea of progress, an idea that nourishes only the false consolation that what may have happened in the past could not possibly happen again. "The current amazement that the things we are experiencing are 'still' possible in the twentieth century is *not* philosophical." But his disdain for progress has the curious consequence of making all historical action appear meaningless. The historical materialist, he insists, must not subscribe to the myth that the modest efforts we perform now might contribute gradually to future improvement. The historical materialist must instead recognize that *all* of history is catastrophe. Revolution will come not through working *within* the historical continuum. It will demand a "leap in the open air" that will liberate humanity from the ruins.[27]

The image of "the angel of history" raises many questions but offers few answers. What does such a revolution consist in? And who is expected to act? In Klee's painting, the angel appears as if it were merely hovering in a void. But this was hardly an encouragement to realistic action. In Benjamin's interpretation, the angel seems to be less an agent of history than its victim: it is caught by its wings in a storm that it is unable to control. If this is meant to convey a species of political theology, it is altogether different from Carl Schmitt's political theology of willful decision that Benjamin had once found inspiring. The angel has little authority and apparently no powers of action. Like a melancholy prince, it appears to be at the mercy of historical events and can only look backward with longing to an irrecoverable past.

At the end of his theses, Benjamin appended two sections, both of which he left unnumbered and omitted from later drafts. In the second section he refers to the Jewish conception of time:

> We know that the Jews were prohibited from inquiring into the future: the Torah and the prayers instructed them in remembrance [*Eingedenken*]. This disenchanted the future, which holds sway over all those who turn to soothsayers for enlightenment. This does not imply, however, that for the Jews the future became homogeneous, empty time. For every second was the small gateway in time through which the Messiah might enter.[28]

Although we may never learn why Benjamin omitted this passage, it could be that he finally came to recognize the paradox at the heart of his thinking. Ever since the early 1920s he had sought to bring politics and theology into a workable combination. The result, however, was always unstable. Like Goethe, it seemed as if he were experimenting with chemical elements that created not a true synthesis but only a volatile compound. In his final experiment, he sought to unite Marxism with messianism. Once again, however, the experiment threatened to go awry.

The difficulty was that the two elements were essentially at odds. No doubt Benjamin would never have wished to declare himself a proponent of Marxist orthodoxy, but he knew enough about Marxism to grasp its basic claims. It is an essential principle of historical materialism that all changes in history must emerge from contradictions that are immanent to history itself. In the theses, however, Benjamin violated this principle. The "messianic" appeared as a contradictory force that intrudes upon history as if from the outside. In condemning the bourgeois fetish of historical progress, Benjamin abandoned a theme that is vital to historical materialism. He came to resemble his own beloved angel: he turned his back on the future and yielded to his own melancholic sense that history is a realm of vanity from which nothing better can emerge.

Toward the Sea

In the winter and spring of 1940, he continued to read widely but with a focus on French literature: an exceptionally long letter to Horkheimer provides an overview of his reading, most of which he saw as contributions for his study of the arcades.[29] All the while, however, he was making further preparations for his journey to the United States. By the end of January he had started English lessons, together with Hannah Arendt and her husband Heinrich Blücher. He even reported to Adorno that he was reading William Faulkner's *Light in August*, though he feared that his reading ability still far outstripped his conversational skills.[30]

In early February he had submitted the application for a visa to the American consulate in Bordeaux, though he had learned from others that the system for processing visas was exceptionally slow. In early April he shared with Horkheimer disquieting news about his health: the doctor had diagnosed him with myocarditis and hypertension, and he was obliged to remain at rest in his flat. There were days when "after a hundred steps in the street I am drenched with sweat and cannot go on." In a letter to Stephan Lackner he expressed special worry for the *Angelus Novus*, whose image had helped to inspire his theses on history. "This picture being the sole object of importance and feasible for sale that remains to me, I have the greatest hesitations to part from it for the purposes of funding my everyday expenses. It's precisely the Klee on which I've always relied for the moment when I would be able to reach America." Even in early May, however, he still did not feel much confidence that the time of his departure was near. Over the previous month his heart condition had only grown worse, and among his sole excursions from the apartment were visits to the doctor. The few acquaintances who remained in Paris were obliged to visit him at home.[31]

In the summer of 1940, the historian Marc Bloch wrote a brilliant memoir of this eight-month period, the *drôle de guerre*, or "phoney war" of inertia and inaction while the French state awaited the inevitable.[32] On May 10, less than a year after the invasion of Poland, the German army commenced its westward drive, pressing through the Low Countries and onward into France. By June 14 its forces surged into Paris and the city was occupied. As the army swept through France, Benjamin entrusted a great share of his writings to Georges Bataille, who promised to store them safely in the Bibliothèque Nationale.[33] By June 14, the very day that Paris fell, Benjamin finally left Paris by train in the company of his sister Dora. They made their way southwest to Lourdes at the foothills of the Pyrenees, where they could remain at least for the time being. He found a bedroom for 200 francs. A great many others, mainly refugees from Belgium, filled the town.[34] On July 8 he wrote a brief note to Hannah Arendt, to whom he confided a wry remark: "I would be in a deeper depression than the one by which I am currently gripped if, as bookless as I am, I had not found in the only book I do have the aphorism that is most splendidly appropriate to my current state. 'His Laziness supported him in glory for many years in the obscurity of an errant and hidden life.' (La Rochefoucault speaking to Retz)."[35]

On August 2 Benjamin still found himself in Lourdes. To Adorno he described his state of mind. "The complete uncertainty about what the next day and even the next hour will bring has dominated my existence for many weeks. I am condemned to read every newspaper (that now come out on a single sheet of paper) like a summons that has been served on me and to detect in every radio broadcast the voice of a messenger of bad tidings."[36] Adorno was looking into the possibility that Benjamin might secure a post as a guest lecturer at the university in Havana or perhaps in San Domingo, though he confessed to Benjamin that neither option seemed likely. Benjamin learned that a visa for the United States had been deposited for him at the American consulate in Marseilles, and on August 16 he was finally able to take a train eastward across the south of France to the port city. He still lacked an exit visa, though, something that he understood for the moment was impossible.[37] But there were other ways to escape.

Gnädige Frau. "Dear Lady." Before her stood a man with graying hair and thick glasses. "Please forgive the intrusion—I hope this is not an inopportune time." The morning light was still gray, and he had knocked at the door at least twice. Port-Vendres, a fishing village, sits above the Mediterranean, about five hours southwest from Marseilles by train. He had made his way there from Paris, by way of Lourdes, where he and his sister Dora had stayed for several weeks while awaiting their papers of transit. It was the twenty-fifth of September, 1940.

With the guidance of Lisa Fittko, Benjamin, together with a small group of refugees, climbed the hills above Banyuls-sur-Mer, upward through the steep vineyards and along the *route Lister* that winds its way through the Pyrenees, inland and far above the coast. Fittko was surprised that Benjamin was carrying a heavy-looking black briefcase. "It contains my new manuscript," he said. "But why have you brought it along on this scouting trip?" she asked. "Do you know, this briefcase is most important to me," he explained. "The manuscript *must* be saved. It is more important than I am."[38] After many hours they came to the summit. From there the path stretched onward and down to the town of Portbou, where they would be required to register in the border office. Beyond lay the blue-green waters of the Mediterranean Sea, flashing in the sun like a promise of freedom.

AFTERWORD

No individual's life is defined by its end. Walter Benjamin's life has been told many times, and even to non-specialists many of the details are well known. In this book I have aimed to provide the reader with a biography that is accessible and faithful to the sources, but I have also tried to conclude the story at a moment when its protagonist did not yet recognize that this would be its conclusion, a moment when he might have still felt a sense of possibility. This has meant making the end into a prologue. In shifting the temporal order of events, I trust the reader will not accuse me of literary gymnastics or willful revisionism. My purpose, however quixotic, has been to honor Benjamin's own desideratum that history should not be written by the victors but brushed "against the grain," as a reminder that at any moment even the smallest change might have turned one's life in a direction one may never have anticipated. Benjamin found his own language to express this hope: Every instant in time can be the gateway through which the Messiah might enter.

Conventions of biographical prose would seem to dictate that one must narrate a life by beginning with birth and ending with death. But the record of human events has turned this convention into a brutal cliché, as if death were the final meaning of life and its higher purpose. The horrors of the mid-twentieth century, or perhaps the horrors of *all* human history, may seem to confirm this truism. Among philosophers, too, this idea has gained a semblance of profundity, not least because the notion of being-toward-death found a zealous advocate in Martin Heidegger, whose work was elevated into the philosophical canon around the same time that Benjamin was expelled. (The attentive reader will take note of a further irony, that as young men both Heidegger and Benjamin had studied in the very same seminar in Heidelberg.)

Some may feel convinced that history always brings closure of some kind, for the simple reason that some possibilities are realized while others are not. I have never found this historicist principle at all convincing. We are stirred by works of literature long after their authors have died, and we find ourselves moved by symphonies whose significance is not bound to the time when they were composed. Benjamin, perhaps more than most professional historians, was alive to the enigma that works of the past offer more riches than the past can control. This is no less true of an individual life. In violating a narrative convention, I have tried to undo the historicist cliché by restoring some measure of contingency to a human life that, like all lives, remains forever open in its meaning. I have therefore left Benjamin poised above the sea, at a moment when he was not yet certain whether he would be among the drowned or the saved.

In her introduction to *Illuminations*, the first English-language anthology of Benjamin's prose, first published in 1968,

Hannah Arendt observed that the death of her friend at the Spanish border was a result, at least in part, of the sheer fact of bad timing: "A few weeks later the embargo on visas was lifted again. One day earlier Benjamin would have got through without any trouble; one day later the people in Marseilles would have known that for the time being it was impossible to pass through Spain. Only on that particular day was the catastrophe possible."[1] This remark alerts us to the intriguing question of how we should think about counterfactuals, a question that is relevant not only to Benjamin's life but to human experience in all its forms.[2]

In the case of Benjamin, speculations in a counterfactual mode now form a genre unto itself. I refer the reader to an essay by the art historian T. J. Clark that poses the question, "Should Benjamin Have Read Marx?"[3] Although I do not wish to add another title to this genre, I am partial to the moral animus that inspires it. No doubt many critics may be inclined to disparage counterfactual speculation as little more than a parlor game, one that is best left, perhaps, to amateur military historians and war enthusiasts, for whom history is a record of strategies taken or not taken. But there is little reason to take sides with the professionals. The Second World War in particular has inspired counterfactual reasoning, not only among historians but also among novelists. To take only one prominent example, Philip Roth's novel *The Plot Against America* left many readers shaken regarding the durability of democratic institutions in the United States. We should find it not irresponsible but instructive when we set the imagination free to consider possibilities that were not strictly the case.

The life of Walter Benjamin raises a host of counterfactual questions. But most of them are bent toward a single concern, like light in the presence of an overwhelming mass. Who would he have been and where would he have been had he survived? My suspicion is that, unlike Scholem, who urged him to come to Jerusalem, he would not have felt at ease in Zion. Early in his life Benjamin was drawn to the utopian promises of the Jugendbewegung, but when he broke away from the youth movement he did so because he had grown disillusioned with the bellicose aspect of group belonging. Especially after the horrors of the First World War, nationalism in all its forms repelled him. It is therefore hard to imagine that he could have embraced the State of Israel, given that the imperative of its survival has required a Faustian bargain with power even in its most brutal forms.[4] Nor is it plausible to think that an intellectual so reluctant to accept the imperatives of in-group loyalty would have felt stirrings of commitment to another solidaristic collective.

For the very same reasons, however, it is surely relevant to note that Benjamin never joined the Communist party. Had he done so, and had he moved to Moscow, in all probability he would have soon grown disillusioned, and he would have suffered the persecution that was visited upon nearly all dissidents in the Soviet Union. It is far easier, I think, to imagine that Benjamin might have passed without difficulty through Portbou. He might have arrived a day earlier or a day later—either option is available, since in our minds we are free to choose—and then he could have boarded a ship in Lisbon to cross the Atlantic. Perhaps he would have remained in Cuba for several months or years. Eventually he might have made his way to the United States, where he could have joined members of the Institute for Social Research at its offices in Morningside Heights. Or, and this is just as likely, he might have ended up on the Lower East Side as the owner of an antiquarian bookshop, not unlike his son Stefan, who seems to have inherited his father's bibliophilic habits and, after the war, ended up as a bookseller in London.

A further problem confronts most biographers. The more closely one examines the life of an intellectual or an artist, the more likely one will find confirmation for the inconvenient truth:

genius seldom goes together with personal virtue. This is surely the case for any biography of Walter Benjamin. In this book I have chosen not to dwell on the less palatable aspects of his character—his gambling, his infidelities, his erratic moods, or his penchant for ruthlessly cutting off friendships when they no longer suited his needs. It is an unfortunate fact that in human life flaws of personal character are not the exception but the rule.

There is a final question that perhaps deserves consideration: does it make sense in the end to categorize the life of Walter Benjamin within the larger genre of Jewish lives? To this question I have no certain answer. Benjamin was first and foremost an intellectual, a literary and cultural theorist whose mind ranged freely across a broad terrain, seldom stopping to ask himself whether he had the requisite papers of transit for other lands. Through the practice of interpretation he made everything his own. What he knew of Judaism in his childhood was little more than a paucity of rituals or allusions, and what he learned as an adult came chiefly from his friendship with Gershom Scholem, whose knowledge was vast and deep. What Benjamin did with this learning, however, was no different than what he did with anything he found. He brought it up, like a pearl from the ocean floor, and he polished it, again and again, until it shone as brilliantly as a star. Although his death was no doubt tragic, I prefer to remember him as he was in life: hidden away in the library, searching for half-forgotten treasure.

REFERENCES

AB Theodor Adorno and Walter Benjamin, *The Complete Correspondence, 1928–1940*, edited by Henri Lonitz, translated by Nicholas Walker (Cambridge: Harvard University Press, 2001).

AP Walter Benjamin, *The Arcades Project*, translated by Howard Eiland and Kevin McLaughlin; originally edited by Rolf Tiedemann (Cambridge: Harvard University Press, 1999).

BB Erdmut Wizisla, *Benjamin and Brecht: The Story of a Friendship* (London: Verso, 2016).

BC Walter Benjamin, *A Berlin Childhood Around 1900*, translated by Howard Eiland (Cambridge: Harvard University Press, 2006).

BW Bernd Witte, *Walter Benjamin: An Intellectual Biography*, translated by James Rolleston (Detroit: Wayne State University Press, 1991).

CB Walter Benjamin, *The Correspondence of Walter Benjamin*,

1910–1940, edited by Gershom Scholem and Theodor W. Adorno, translated by Manfred R. Jacobson and Evelyn M. Jacobson (Chicago: University of Chicago Press, 1994).

CC *The Cambridge Companion to Walter Benjamin*, edited by David Ferris (Cambridge: Cambridge University Press, 2004).

CW Charlotte Wolff, *On the Way to Myself: Communications to a Friend* (London: Methuen, 1969).

EJ Howard Eiland and Michael Jennings, *Walter Benjamin: A Critical Life* (Cambridge: Harvard University Press, 2014).

EW Walter Benjamin, *Early Writings, 1910–1917*, translated by Howard Eiland et al. (Cambridge: Harvard University Press, 2011).

GB Walter Benjamin, *Gesammelte Briefe*, edited by Christoph Gödde and Henri Lonitz (Suhrkamp Verlag, 1995).
Volume 1: 1910–1918
Volume 2: 1919–1924
Volume 3: 1925–1930
Volume 4: 1931–1934
Volume 5: 1935–1937
Volume 6: 1938–1940

GE Walter Benjamin, *Gedichte und Erzählungen*, edited by Chryssoula Kambas, in volume 5 of Walter Benjamin, *Werke und Nachlaß, Kritische Gesamtausgabe* (Suhrkamp, 2024).

GS Walter Benjamin, *Gesammelte Schriften*, assisted by Theodor W. Adorno and Gershom Scholem, edited by Rolf Tiedemann and Hermann Schweppenhäuser (Suhrkamp, 1977–).

LF Lisa Fittko, *Escape Through the Pyrenees*, translated by David Koblick (Chicago: Northwestern University Press, 1991).

LY Gershom Scholem, *Lamentations of Youth: The Diaries of*

Gershom Scholem, 1913–1919, edited and translated by Anthony David Skinner (Cambridge: Harvard University Press, 2007).

MB Momme Brodersen, *Walter Benjamin: A Biography*, translated by Malcolm R. Green and Ingrida Ligers (London: Verso, 1998).

MD Walter Benjamin, *Moscow Diary*, edited by Gary Smith, translated by Richard Sieburth (Cambridge: Harvard University Press, 1986).

NF Carina Birman, *The Narrow Foothold* (London: Hearing Eye, 2006).

OB Gary Smith, editor, *On Walter Benjamin: Critical Essays and Recollections* (Cambridge: MIT Press, 1988).

OS Walter Benjamin, *One-Way Street*, edited by Michael Jennings, translated by Edmund Jephcott (Cambridge: Harvard University Press, 2016).

OT Walter Benjamin, *Origin of the German Trauerspiel*, translated by Howard Eiland (Cambridge: Harvard University Press, 2019).

SB *The Correspondence of Walter Benjamin and Gershom Scholem, 1932–1940*, translated by Gary Smith and Andre Lefevere (New York: Schocken, 1989).

SF Gershom Scholem, *Walter Benjamin: The Story of a Friendship*, translated by Harry Zohn (New York: Schocken, [1988], © 1981).

SW Walter Benjamin, *Selected Writings* (Cambridge: Harvard University Press, 1996–).

Volume 1: 1913–1926, edited by Marcus Bullock and Michael W. Jennings

Volume 2: 1927–1934, edited by Michael W. Jennings, Howard Eiland, and Gary Smith

Volume 3: 1935–1938, edited by Howard Eiland and Michael W. Jennings

Volume 4: 1938–1940, edited by Howard Eiland and Michael W. Jennings

WM Walter Benjamin, *The Writer on Modern Life: Essays on Charles Baudelaire* edited by Michael Jennings (Cambridge: Harvard University Press, 2006).

Other Works of Interest

For those who are interested in further understanding Benjamin's life and work, the following studies may prove helpful.

Esther Leslie, *Walter Benjamin: Overpowering Conformism* (London: Pluto, 2000).

Eva Weissweiler, *Villa Verde oder das Hotel in San Remo: Das italienische Exil der Familie Benjamin* (btb Verlag, 2022).

Eva Weissweiler, *Das Echo deiner Frage: Dora und Walter Benjamin—Biographie einer Beziehung* (Hamburg: Hoffmann und Campe, 2020).

Eva Weissweiler, *Lisa Fittko: Biographie einer Fluchthelferin* (Hamburg: Hoffmann und Campe, 2024).

Max Pensky, *Melancholy Dialectics: Walter Benjamin and the Play of Mourning* (Amherst: University of Massachusetts Press, 1993).

Walter Benjamin's Archive: Images, Texts, Signs, edited by Ursula Marx, Michael Schwartz, Gudrun Schwarz, and Erdmut Wizisla, translated by Esther Leslie (London: Verso, 2015).

Radio Benjamin, edited by Lecia Rosenthal (London: Verso, 2014).

Eli Friedländer, *Walter Benjamin: A Philosophical Portrait* (Cambridge: Harvard University Press, 2014).

Frederic Jameson, *The Benjamin Files* (London: Verso, 2022).

Carolin Duttlinger, editor, with Ben Morgan and Anthony Phelan, *Walter Benjamins Anthopologisches Denken*, Rombach Litterae (Freiburg i. Br.: Rombach, 2012).

Esther Leslie, *Walter Benjamin*, Critical Lives series (London: Reaktion, 2007).

NOTES

Prologue

1. For a detailed biography, see Eva Weissweiler, *Lisa Fittko: Biographie einer Fluchthelferin.*
2. See the description in SF, 9.
3. LF, 103.
4. LF, 106.
5. LF, 108.
6. LF, 111.
7. LF, 113.
8. NF, 5.
9. EJ, 676; MB, 261.
10. SF, 226.

Chapter 1. A Berlin Childhood

1. BC, 99.
2. BW, 2.

3. On the distinction between acculturation and assimilation, see Jonathan Frankel, "Assimilation and the Jews of Nineteenth-Century Europe: Towards a New Historiography?" in *Assimilation and Community: The Jews in Nineteenth-Century Europe*, ed. Jonathan Frankel and Steven J. Zipperstein (Cambridge: Cambridge University Press, 1992), 1–37.

4. *Düsseldorfer Heine-Ausgabe*, volume 10: *Shakespeares Mädchen und Frauen und kleinere literaturkritische Schriften* (1993), S. 313.

5. EJ, 20.

6. CB (Letter 193, To Gershom Scholem, January 20, 1930), 358–360, quote from 359.

7. See SF, 18; RW, 1; also see L. Rosenthal, "Simeon van Geldern, Heinrich Heine's Famous Great-Uncle in Holland," *Studia Rosenthaliana* 6, no. 2 (July 1972): 180–203. Also D. Kaufmann, *Aus Heinrich Heine's Ahnensaal* (1896); and G. Wilhelm, ed., *Heine Bibliographie* (1960).

8. SF, 64.

9. SW, 2:597–598.

10. BC, 80.

11. BC, 81.

12. On Benjamin and stamp collecting, see Martin Jay, "Timbremelancholy: Walter Benjamin and the Fate of Philately," *Journal of Comparative Literature and Aesthetics* 42, no. 2 (2019): 10–19.

13. HA, 38, 45.

14. Michael A. Meyer, *Response to Modernity: A History of the Reform Movement in Judaism* (Detroit: Wayne State University Press, 1988), 97.

15. BC, 123–124.

16. GB, 159n ("Erwägungen"). Also see the version in English, BC, 25n3.

17. BC, 124.

18. On this theme see Peter E. Gordon, *Migrants in the Profane: Critical Theory and the Question of Secularization* (New Haven: Yale University Press, 2020).

19. Gershom Scholem, "Walter Benjamin," *The Leo Baeck Me-*

morial Lecture 9 (New York: Leo Baeck Institute, 1965), 5–24, quote from 16.

20. MB, 20, and see 268n5.

21. See the statistics in *Jews in Nazi Berlin: From Kristallnacht to Liberation*, edited by Beate Meyer, Hermann Simon, and Chana Schütz (Chicago: University of Chicago Press, 2009). Also see Gerd Hohorst, Jürgen Kocka, and Gerhard A. Ritter, *Sozialgeschichtliches Arbeitsbuch II*, 2nd ed. (Munich: Beck, 1978), 42–44.

22. MB, 20.

23. MB, 13.

24. BC, 58–60, 135, 137.

25. SW, 2:597.

26. MB, 7.

27. BC, 49.

28. BC, 134.

29. BC, 158, 159, 67.

30. BC, 67.

31. BC, 68.

Chapter 2. Youth and Utopia

1. "Experience," SW, 1:3–5, quote from 5.

2. Richard Dougherty, "Eros, Youth Culture, and *Geist*" (Ph.D. dissertation, University of Wisconsin, Madison, 1978), 9.

3. Shulamith Volkov, "Anti-Semitism as a Cultural Code," *Leo Baeck Institute Year Book* 23 (1978): 25–45.

4. For a general history, see Peter D. Stachura, *The German Youth Movement, 1900–1945: An Interpretive and Documentary History* (London: Macmillan, 1981).

5. Dougherty, "Eros, Youth Culture, and *Geist*," 9. A representative selection of Wyneken's speeches can be found in Gustav Wyneken, *Der Kampf für die Jugend: Gesammelte Aufsätze* (Jena: Eugen Diederichs Verlag, 1919).

6. Dougherty, "Eros, Youth Culture, and *Geist*," 11.

7. Dougherty, "Eros, Youth Culture, and *Geist*," 11.

8. Jörg Wollenberg, "Vom 'Haubinder Judenkrach' über die Odenwaldschule: Theodor Lessing erblickte in den Landerzie-

hungsheimen eine unerschöpfliche Quelle pädagogischer Ideen und setzte auf Aufklärung und nicht auf Weltflucht," *Frankfurter Allgemeine Zeitung* (September 2, 2010).

9. Paul Reitter, *On the Origins of Jewish Self-Hatred* (Princeton: Princeton University Press, 2012).

10. Sander Gilman, *Jewish Self-Hatred: Anti-Semitism and the Hidden Language of the Jews* (Baltimore: Johns Hopkins University Press, 1990); Michael Berkowitz, *Zionist Culture and West European Jewry Before the First World War* (Cambridge: Cambridge University Press, 1993).

11. "Der Dichter," in GE, 5:9–10; my translation.

12. For a general summary, see Steven Aschheim, "1912: The Publication of Moritz Goldstein's 'The German-Jewish Parnassus' Sparks a Debate over Assimilation, German-Culture, and the 'Jewish Spirit,'" in *The Yale Companion to Jewish Writing and Thought in German Culture, 1096–1996*, edited by Sander L. Gilman and Jack Zipes (New Haven: Yale University Press, 1997), 299–305.

13. Franz Quentin (a pseudonym for Ludwig Strauss), "Sprechsaal, Aussprache zur Judenfrage," *Der Kunstwart* 25, no. 22 (August 2, 1912): 243 and ff. A small excerpt from this essay can be found in *Benjaminiana*, edited by Hans Puttnies and Gary Smith (Giessen: Anabas Verlag, 1991), 39–54.

14. *Benjaminiana*, edited by Hans Puttnies and Gary Smith (Giessen: Anabas Verlag, 1991), 45.

15. GB (Letter 23, September 11, 1912), 1:61–62.

16. GB (Letter 23, September 11, 1912), 1:62.

17. GB (Letter 23, September 11, 1912), 1:62. The phrase is Benjamin's own; but he is paraphrasing a passage by Heinrich Mann, published in the volume *Judentaufen*, edited by Werner Sombart (München, 1912), 69. "Wenn kein Jude mehr das öffentliche Leben ein wenig geistiger macht, und kein Judin mehr die Liebe? Die Folgen der vollständigen Assimilierung und die Trennung wären gleich schauderhaft." Quoted in the notes to GB (Letter 23, September 11, 1912), 1:68.

18. GB (Letter 23, September 11, 1912), 1:62, emphasis added.

19. GB (Letter 24, October 10, 1912), 1:69.

20. GB (Letter 24, October 10, 1912), 1:70. Hegelian themes in Benjamin's thought, however, are noticeably rare. On his Nietzschean inheritance, see James McFarland, *Constellation: Friedrich Nietzsche and Walter Benjamin in the Now-Time of History* (New York: Fordham University Press, 2012).

21. GB (Letter 23, September 11, 1912), 1:64; GB (Letter 24, October 10, 1912), 1:71, emphasis added.

22. On Benjamin and Ahad Ha'am, see SF, 29. For a deeper treatment of Ahad Ha'am and "cultural Zionism," see Steven J. Zipperstein, *Elusive Prophet: Ahad Ha'am and the Origins of Zionism* (Berkeley and Los Angeles: University of California Press, 1993).

23. GB (Letter 26, January 7, 1914), 1:82–83; GB (Letter 25, November 12, 1912), 1:75; GB (Letter 24, October 10, 1912), 1:71.

24. BC (Letter 10, April 29, 1913), 18.

25. "The Metaphysics of Youth," SW, 1:6–17, quote from 10.

26. BC (Letter 24, August 4, 1913), 49.

27. Betty Falkenberg, *Else Lasker-Schüler: A Life* (Jefferson, N.C.: McFarland, 2003).

28. As quoted in Emanuela Barasch Rubinstein, *Mephisto in the Third Reich: Literary Representations of Evil in Nazi Germany;* see especially chapter 3, "I and I by Else Lasker-Schüler," 71–96. See also Benny Ziffer, "The Kiss of July," *Haaretz*, July 16, 2010; and Ruth Schwertfeger, *Else Lasker-Schüler: Inside This Deathly Solitude* (Bloomsbury Academic, 1991).

29. Shachar Pinsker, "A Modern (Jewish) Woman in a Café: Leah Goldberg and the Poetic Space of the Coffeehouse," *Jewish Social Studies*, new series, volume 21, number 1 (Fall 2015): 1–48.

30. MB, 69. Brodersen is quoting Bernhard Reichenbach, "'Kriegsfreiwilliger' Benjamin," in *Die Zeit* (March 10, 1967), 29.

31. MB, 69.

32. Gustav Wyneken, "Der Krieg und die Jugend" (öffentlicher Vortrag gehalten am 25. November 1914 in der Münchner Freien), 19.

33. CB (Letter 39, March 9, 1915), 75–76.

34. "The Life of Students," SW, 1:37–47, quotes from 39, 37–38.

Chapter 3. From War to Peace

1. Lewis D. Wurgaft, *The Activists: Kurt Hiller and the Politics of Action on the German Left, 1914–1933* (Philadelphia: American Philosophical Society, 1977).

2. On Scholem's trajectory, see his memoir, Gershom Scholem, *Von Berlin nach Jerusalem* (Ausgabe, 2016); for a biographical account see David Biale, *Gershom Scholem: Master of the Kabbalah* (New Haven: Yale University Press, 2018); for an analysis of Scholem's scholarship, see David Biale, *Gershom Scholem: Kabbalah and Counter-History* (Cambridge: Harvard University Press, 1979).

3. SF, 5.

4. SF, 3–4.

5. SF, 6–7.

6. SF, 17–18. Also see CB, 77.

7. LY, 168.

8. Michael Brenner, *The Renaissance of Jewish Culture in Weimar Germany* (New Haven: Yale University Press, 1998).

9. *Der Jude: Eine Monatsschrift* (Berlin: R. Löwit Verlag, 1916–1917).

10. Martin Buber, "Die Losung," in *Der Jude: Eine Monatsschrift* (1916), 1–3, quote from 2.

11. CB (Letter 45, To Martin Buber, July 1916), 79–81.

12. CB (Letter 45, To Martin Buber, July 1916), 79–81.

13. SF, 28.

14. For a contemporary summary of *Erlebnisphilosophie* along with other currents of philosophy in the first decades of the twentieth century, see Fritz Heinemann, *Neue Wege der Philosophie: Geist, Leben, Existenz* (Leibzig: Quelle und Meyer, 1929). For a modern survey of debates over the meaning of "experience," see Martin Jay, *Songs of Experience: Modern European and American Variations on a Universal Theme* (Berkeley: University of California Press, 2005).

15. SF, 29.

16. "On Language as Such and on the Language of Man," SW, 1:62–74, quotes from 68, 71–74.

17. On the theme of natural history in Benjamin's work, see the extraordinarily insightful study by Beatrice Hanssen, *Walter*

Benjamin's Other History: Of Stones, Animals, Human Beings, and Angels (Berkeley: University of California Press, 2000).

18. For more on nominalism in general and Benjamin's place in the broader discourse of nominalism, see Martin Jay, *Magical Nominalism: The Historical Event, Aesthetic Reenchantment, and the Photograph* (Chicago: University of Chicago Press, 2025).

19. "On the Mimetic Faculty" (1933), SW, 2:722.

20. SF, 32. The phrase may strike some readers as an unambiguous endorsement of Judaism. Still, it should be noted that Scholem does not quote Benjamin directly; he quotes from his own diary, in which he had apparently recorded, or paraphrased, Benjamin's words.

21. "On the Concept of History" (1940), SW, 4:389–400, quote from 390.

22. "On Language as Such and on the Language of Man," in SW, 1:62–74, quote from 70.

23. "On the Program of the Coming Philosophy," in SW, 1:100–110, quote from 110; see also 110n4 on the meaning on the term *Lehre* (or "teaching"), which Benjamin used at this time, partly thanks to the influence of Scholem, who wrote: "In those years—between 1915 and at least 1927—the religious sphere assumed a central importance for Benjamin that was utterly removed from fundamental doubt. At its center was the concept of *Lehre* [teaching], which for him included the philosophical realm but definitely transcended it." SF, 55.

24. On Grete Radt, see EW, 221n1; and CB, 60–62.

25. EW, 214–223.

26. *Theodor Herzl's Lehrjahre* (1920); *Theodor Herzl's Zionistische Schriften* (1908). For more on the life of Leon Kellner, see David Rechter, *At Eden's Door: The Habsburg Jewish Life of Leon Kellner, 1859–1928* (London: Littman Library of Jewish Civilization in association with Liverpool University Press, 2023).

27. For the full story of their relationship, see Eva Weissweiler, *Das Echo deiner Frage: Dora und Walter Benjamin—Biographie einer Beziehung.*

28. CB (Letter 31, May 6, 1914), 60.

29. EJ, 91; MB, 93.
30. GB, 1:356, 369.
31. EJ, 98; GB, 1:441.
32. From Scholem's unpublished diary (December 17, 1917), as quoted in *Benjaminiana*, 57.
33. GB, 1:449.
34. BC (Letter 67, To Gerhard Scholem, April 17, 1918), 123.
35. SF, 76.
36. SF, 58. Scholem uses the alternative title "Warder" rather than "Warden." I have silently changed the title here for Anglophone readers.
37. SF, 58.
38. SW, 1:103.
39. SW, 1:117, 118.
40. SW, 1:134–135, 146, 151, 152.
41. SW, 1:159, 152. For an explanation of this idea, see Rebecca Comay, "Benjamin and the Ambiguities of Romanticism," in CC, 134–151 esp. 148.
42. SW, 1:161, 185; emphasis added.
43. MB, 104.
44. CB (Letter 193, To Scholem, January 20, 1930), 359.

Chapter 4. Angelus Novus

1. MB, 132.
2. CB (Letter 88, To Gershom Scholem, February 13, 1920), 160.
3. CB (Letter 90, To Gershom Scholem, May 26, 1920), 163.
4. CB (Letter 90, To Gershom Scholem, May 26, 1920), 164.
5. Georg Lukács, "Über den Dostojewski-Nachlass," *Moskauer Rundschau* (March 22, 1931). For a discussion of this term and its historical application to Lukács's own pre-Marxist writing, see Michael Löwy, "Naphta or Settembrini? Lukács and Romantic Anticapitalism," *New German Critique*, no. 42 (Autumn 1987): 17–31. For a more comprehensive view, see Michael Löwy, *Georg Lukács: From Romanticism to Bolshevism* (London: New Left Books,

1979), 15–30. For the expressionism debate between Lukács and Bloch in relation to romantic anti-capitalism, see Ferenc Fehér, "The Last Phase of Romantic Anti-Capitalism: Lukács' Response to the War," *New German Critique*, no. 10 (Winter 1977): 139–154. For a general portrait of Jewish intellectuals and romantic anti-capitalism, see Michael Löwy, *Redemption and Utopia: Jewish Libertarian Thought in Central Europe* (Athlone Press, 1992).

6. Georg Lukács, *The Theory of the Novel*, Anna Bostok, trans. (Cambridge: MIT Press, 1971), 29, as quoted in Löwy, "Naphta or Settembrini? Lukács and Romantic Anticapitalism," 19.

7. See Löwy, "Naphta or Settembrini? Lukács and Romantic Anticapitalism," 18–19.

8. Ernst Bloch, *The Spirit of Utopia*, Anthony A. Nassar, trans. (Stanford University Press, 2000), 3.

9. Bloch, *The Spirit of Utopia*, 276, emphasis added.

10. Bloch, *The Spirit of Utopia*, 278.

11. See CB (Letter 82, To Ernst Schoen, September 19, 1919), 148.

12. CB (Letter 82, To Ernst Schoen, September 19, 1919), 148.

13. "Theological-Political Fragment," SW, 3:305–306, quote from 305.

14. "Theological-Political Fragment," SW, 3:305–306. On the dispute over the proper dating of the text see the editors' remarks at 306n1.

15. Georges Sorel, *Reflections on Violence*, edited by Jeremy Jennings, *Cambridge Texts of the History of Political Thought* (Cambridge: Cambridge University Press, 1999).

16. "Critique of Violence," SW, 1:236–252, 249–50.

17. "Critique of Violence," SW, 1:236–252, 250.

18. Scholem, "Walter Benjamin and His Angel," 62. The suggestion that the painting served as an "object of meditation" is quoted from 62.

19. Scholem, "Walter Benjamin and His Angel," 64; also see CB (Letter 102, August 4, 1921), 185–186.

20. "Announcement of the Journal *Angelus Novus*," SW, 2:262–

296, quotes from 293, 295, 294, 296. German from "Ankündigung der Zeitschrift: Angelus Novus," GS, volume 2, part 1, 241–246.

21. "Announcement of the Journal *Angelus Novus*," SW, quote from 2:296. My translation modified from the German from "Ankündigung der Zeitschrift: Angelus Novus," GS, volume 2, part 1, 241–246.

22. MB, 120.

23. SF, 104–105.

24. CB, 199–201.

25. CW, 194.

26. CW, 195.

27. CB, 201.

28. On Hofmannsthal's journal, see Alys X. George, "Editing Interwar Europe: *The Dial* and *Neue Deutsche Beiträge*," *Austrian Studies* 23 (2015): 16–34.

29. CB (Letter 100, To Scholem, July 20, 1921), 182; CB (Letter 108, To Scholem, November 27, 1921), 196.

30. "Goethe's Elective Affinities," SW, 1:297–360, quotes from 296, 297, 298, 324, 326.

31. "Goethe's Elective Affinities," SW, 1:297–360, 334.

32. "Goethe's Elective Affinities," SW, 1:297–360, 342.

33. "Goethe's Elective Affinities," SW, 1:297–360, quotes from 334, 339, 351.

34. "Goethe's Elective Affinities," SW, 1:297–360, quotes from 341, 355. See also Paula Schwebel, "Intensive Infinity: Walter Benjamin's Reception of Leibniz," *Modern Language Notes* 127, no. 3 (2012): 589–610.

35. Max Weber, "Science as a Vocation," Rodney Livingstone, trans., David Owen and Tracy B. Strong, eds. (Hackett, 2004), 7. I have modified the translation slightly.

36. CB, 202.

37. EJ, 178; MB, 133.

38. CB, 204, 261.

39. OT, Appendix A, 261–270.

40. OT, Appendix A, all quotes from 261 and *passim*.

41. OT, 36. German quoted from GS, volume 1, part 1, 235.

In Eiland's translation, the German *Verfall* is translated both as "decadence" and "decline."

42. OT, 37.

43. Carl Schmitt, *Political Theology: Four Chapters on the Theory of Sovereignty*, George Schwab, trans. (Chicago: University of Chicago Press, 1985), 89.

44. On the analogy between sovereign decision and miracles, see Sandrine Baume, "Emancipation from the Legal Order: Carl Schmitt and Hans Kelsen on the Use and Misuse of the Miracle Analogy," *The Political Science Reviewer* 46, no. 1 (2022): 209–238.

45. Schmitt, *Political Theology*, 5.

46. GB (Letter 700, To Carl Schmitt, December 9, 1930), 3:558. The reference to Schmitt's study of dictatorship is Carl Schmitt, *Die Diktatur: Von den Anfängen des modernen Souveranitätsdankens bis zum proletarischen Klassenkampf*, 2 Aufl. mit einem Anhang, "Die Diktatur des Reichspräsidenten nach Art. 48 der Weimarer Verfassung" (Munich/Leipzig, 1928). The original edition of the book was first published in 1921, but the editors of Benjamin's correspondence do not reference the original. It is possible that Benjamin only knew of the later edition.

47. Carl Schmitt, *Hamlet oder Hekuba* (Düsseldorf/Köln: Eugen Diederichs Verlag, 1956), esp. 62–67.

48. OT, 67, 189, 145, 163.

49. OT, 254.

50. For the "turnabout" (*Umschwung*), see OT, 254; GS, volume 1, part 1, 406.

51. OT, 254; GS, volume 1, part 1, 405; Eiland's translation modified.

52. The German for "holy translation" is "Heil der Rettung." See OT, 254; GS, volume 1, part 1, 405.

53. EJ, 190.

54. MB, 134.

55. On the importance of this period, see Martin Mittelmeier, *Naples, 1925: Adorno, Benjamin, and the Summer That Made Critical Theory*, Shelley Frisch, trans. (New Haven: Yale University Press, 2024).

56. CB (Letter to Scholem, February 19, 1925), 261.
57. The details are recounted in MB, 147.
58. As quoted in EJ, 231.
59. EJ, 233.
60. CB (Letter to Scholem, July 21, 1925), 276.
61. CB (Letter to Scholem, July 21, 1925), 278.

Chapter 5. The Wanderer

1. GB (Letter 453, To Jula Cohn, September 7, 1925), 3:81. A translation of this same passage also appeared in EJ, 240–241. The translation here is my own.
2. "The Task of the Translator," SW, 1:253–263, quotes from 257, 262.
3. GB, 3:67, 62, 63; also see the editorial note on 42. Also see BC, 267.
4. CB, 277.
5. MB, 161.
6. "Traumkitsch," GS, volume 2, part 2, 620–622.
7. "Naples," SW, 1:414–421, quotes from 417 and *passim.*
8. On Lacis, see Liga Ulberte, "Anna Lacis and Bernhard Reich: Life and Love in the Theater," *Canadian Review of Comparative Literature/Revue Canadienne de Littérature Comparée* (March 2018): 51–68. Also see Susan Ingram, "The Writing of Asja Lacis," *New German Critique* 86 (2002): 159–177.
9. MB, 158.
10. OS, 72.
11. OS, 76–77.
12. SF, 140.
13. CB, 287–288.
14. OS, 57.
15. CB, 292–293.
16. GB (Letter to Siegfried Kracauer, July 15, 1926), 3:182.
17. CB, 297.
18. CB, 201, 202.
19. EJ, 263–264.

20. CB, 307.

21. GB (Letter to Gershom Scholem, September 10, 1926), 3:187.

22. Gershom Scholem, "Walter Benjamin," *The Leo Baeck Memorial Lecture* 8 (New York: Leo Baeck Institute, 1965), 5–24, quote from 6.

23. EJ, 267.

24. "Moscow," in SW, 2:22–46, quotes from 27, 26.

25. "Moscow," in SW, 2:22–46, quotes from 38, 39.

26. MD, 72–73, as quoted in SW, 2:824.

27. CB (Letter 161, To Martin Buber, February 23, 1927), 313.

28. The following four paragraphs are reproduced (in modified form and with several editorial cuts) from my essay on Benjamin's radio work, in Peter E. Gordon, "President of the Moon Committee" (a review of *Radio Benjamin*, Verso Books), *Nation*, August 21, 2023.

29. *Walter Benjamin: Exilic Archives*, Yaron David, Mark Joseph, and Noa Shuval, eds. (Tel Aviv Museum of Art, 2015), quote from 38.

30. GB (Letter to Gershom Scholem, November 18, 1927), 3:300–306, editor's note, at 305; and SF, 137.

31. SF, 137.

32. SF, 137, 138.

33. SF, 138, 139.

34. CB, 335. In the English translation the spelling has been modified. For Benjamin's original spelling, see GB (Letter to Gershom Scholem, April 23, 1928), 3:366–370, quote from 367.

35. CB, 338.

36. CB, 339; spelling of the Hebrew as per Benjamin's original letter in German, in GB (Letter to Gershom Scholem, August 1, 1928) 3:403–409.

37. CB, 339, 342–343. Also see EJ, 308.

38. CB, 346, 348. On the "School for Jewish Youth," see Yfaat Weiss, "Die deutsche Judenheit im Spiegel ihres Erziehungswesens, 1933–1938," *Zeitschrift für Religions- und Geistesgeschichte* 43, no. 3 (1991): 248–265; for an explanation regarding the Schule der jüdi-

schen Jugend, see esp. 258. My thanks to Derek Penslar for alerting me to this reference.

39. CB, 362–364, quotes from 363.

40. CB (Letter 199, To Scholem, November 3, 1930), 369–370.

41. CB, 365.

42. For the encounter in Naples, see Martin Mittelmeier, *Naples, 1925: Adorno, Benjamin, and the Summer that Made Critical Theory*, Shelly Frisch, trans. (New Haven: Yale University Press, 2024). The emphasis on Naples, though overstated, sheds some original light on the early years of friendship among some of the intellectuals associated with the institute.

43. Theodor Adorno, *Negative Dialektik* (Suhrkamp Verlag, 1966), 353–354, my translation.

44. See, e.g., Michael Rosen, "Adorno, Benjamin, and the Decline of the Aura," in *The Cambridge Companion to Critical Theory*, edited by Fred Rush (Cambridge: Cambridge University Press, 2006), 40–56.

45. Martin Jay, *The Dialectical Imagination: A History of the Frankfurt School and the Institute of Social Research, 1923–1950* (Boston: Little, Brown, 1973), 6.

46. SB (Letter 36, Scholem to Benjamin, October 24, 1933), 83–85, quote from 84.

47. GB (Benjamin to Scholem, July 26, 1932), 4:113; SB (Letter 11, Benjamin to Scholem, January 15, 1933), 26.

48. CB (Letter 136, To Gerhard Scholem, September 16, 1924), 246–251, quote from 248.

49. SF, "Appendix" (Letter to Benjamin, March 30, 1931), 227–230, quotes from 228.

50. On the history of the entire Scholem family, see Jay Howard Geller, *The Scholems: A Story of the German-Jewish Bourgeoisie from Emancipation to Destruction* (Ithaca, N.Y.: Cornell University Press, 2019).

51. SF, "Appendix" (Letter to Benjamin, March 30, 1931), 227–230, quotes from 229.

52. SF, "Appendix" (Letter to Scholem, April 17, 1931), 231–233, quote from 231, emphasis added.

53. GB (Letter 578, February 15, 1928), 3:334.

54. AB (Letter 4, To Adorno, November 10, 1930), 6–8.

55. AB (Letter 5, To Adorno, July 17, 1931), 8–12, quotes from 8–9, emphasis added.

56. Benjamin, "Kavaliersmoral," originally in *Die Literarische Welt* (November 22, 1929); now in GS, volume 4, part 1, 466–468.

57. "Franz Kafka: On the Tenth Anniversary of His Death," SW, 2:794–818.

58. "Franz Kafka: On the Tenth Anniversary of His Death," SW, 2:794–818, quotes from 803.

59. "Franz Kafka: On the Tenth Anniversary of His Death," SW, 2:794–818, quotes from 809, 815, 811. Benjamin is quoting from Willy Haas, *Gestalten der Zeit* (Berlin: Kiepenheuer, 1930).

60. "Franz Kafka: On the Tenth Anniversary of His Death," SW, 2:794–818, quotes from 799, 798.

61. AB (Letter 27, December 17, 1934), 66–73, quote from 66–67.

62. CB (Letter 215, To Gershom Scholem, February 28, 1933), 402–404, quote from 402.

63. CB (Letter 216, To Gershom Scholem, March 20, 1933), 405–406, quote from 406.

64. Hilde Benjamin, *Georg Benjamin: Eine Biographie* (Leipzig: S. Hirzel Verlag, 1977), 210.

Chapter 6. Paris Years

1. Adi Armon, "The Parochialism of Intellectual History: The Case of Günther Anders," *The Leo Baeck Institute Year Book* 62 (January 2017). For an intellectual self-portrait, see Günther Anders, "Mein Judentum," in *Mein Judentum*, edited by Hans Jürgen Schultz (Stuttgart, 1978), 65–66.

2. "Paris Diary," SW, 2:337, as quoted in EJ, 335.

3. CB (Letter 168, To Gershom Scholem, January 30, 1928), 321–325, quote from 322.

4. SB, 28.

5. SB, 31.

6. SB (Letter 18, Letter to Benjamin, April 13, 1933), 38–40, quote from 39.

7. For details on the Villa Verde, see Eva Weissweiler, *Villa Verde oder das Hotel in San Remo: Das italienische Exil der Familie Benjamin.*

8. SB (Letter 19, Letter to Scholem, April 19, 1933), 40–42; see esp. 41.

9. SB (Letter 62, To Scholem, August 4, 1934), 133–134; also see SB (Letter 117, To Scholem, February 4, 1939), 240–243; see esp. Scholem's editorial note 242n11.

10. SB (Letter 46, Letter to Scholem, April 8, 1934), 101–103; see 101n1.

11. CB (Letter 210, Letter to Gretel Adorno, Spring 1932 [undated]), 392–394.

12. Jean Selz, "Benjamin in Ibiza," M. Martin Guiney, trans. [originally "Walter Benjamin á Ibiza," *Les Lettres Nouvelles* 2, no. 11 (January 1954): 11–27], in OB, 353–366, quote from 355–356.

13. CB (Letter 221, Letter to Scholem, June 16, 1933), 415–418, quote from 415.

14. GB (Letter 784, Letter to Gretel Karplus, May 16, 1933), 4:205–211.

15. SB (Letter 30, Benjamin to Scholem, July 31, 1933), 69.

16. According to Howard Eiland and Michael Jennings, Benjamin's application for this fund was not approved; EJ, 423.

17. SB (Letter 31, Benjamin to Scholem, September 1, 1933), 72.

18. "Experience and Poverty," SW, 2:731–736, quote from 735.

19. Ernst Fischer and Stephan Füssel, editors, *Geschichte des deutschen Buchhandels im 19. und 20. Jahrhundert*, part 2 (Berlin, Boston, 2012), 99.

20. Günther Gillessen, *Auf verlorenem Posten: Die Frankfurter Zeitung im Dritten Reich* (Berlin: Siedler Verlag, 1986); Wolfgang Schivelbusch, *Intellektuellendämmerung: Zur Lage der Frankfurter Intelligenz in den zwanziger Jahren* (Frankfurt: Insel Verlag, 1982); and Modris Eksteins, "The Frankfurter Zeitung: Mirror of Weimar Democracy," *Journal of Contemporary History* 6, no. 4 (1971): 3–28.

21. CB, 409.

22. Jay, *The Dialectical Imagination*, 30.

23. CB, 408.

24. Benjamin, "Two Kinds of Popularity: Fundamental Principles for a Radio Play," 369–371, quotes from 369, 370. Originally published in the radio magazine *Rufer und Hörer* (September 1932); now in GS, 4.2, 671–673.

25. Berthold Brecht, *Threepenny Novel*, Desmond I. Vesey, trans., verse translations by Christopher Isherwood (London: Granada, 1981), 169.

26. Quoted in BB, 69. The original quote (not included in the English version of the letter) can be found in GB (Letter 693, November 3, 1930), 3:548–551, quote at 548; my translation.

27. SW, 2:768–782. According to his biographers Howard Eiland and Michael Jennings, the question of whether Benjamin actually delivered the address "remains a mystery." See "Chronology, 1927–1934," SW, 2:853.

28. SW, 2:768–782, quotes from 768, 779.

29. SB (Letter 62, August 4, 1934), 133–134.

30. "Notes from Svendborg," SW, 2:783–791, quotes from 787, 786, 789–790.

31. Brecht, *Journals* (August 9, 1941), John Willett, ed., Hugh Rorrison, trans. (London, 1993), 159, as quoted in BB, 173.

32. "Little History of Photography," SW, 2:507–530, quote from 515.

33. On this theme, see the superb essay by Miriam Bratu Hansen, "Benjamin's Aura," *Critical Inquiry* 34, no. 2 (Winter 2008): 336–375.

34. "The Work of Art in the Age of Its Reproducibility," SW, 3:101–133, quote from 116 and 122.

35. "Theories of German Fascism," SW, 2:312–321.

36. SW, 2:314.

37. BB, 98.

38. SF, Appendix (Letter to Benjamin, May 6, 1931), 233–234, quote from 234.

39. AB (Letter 47, Adorno to Benjamin, March 18, 1936), 127–134, quote from 131.

40. AB (Letter 47, Adorno to Benjamin, March 18, 1936), 127–134, quote from 132.

41. CB (To Gretel Karplus, December 30, 1933), 431–432.

42. EJ, 446. For the work of the *Alliance*, see Laurent Grison, "The *Alliance Israélite Universelle* During the Dark Years," *Archives Juives* 34, no. 1 (2001): 9–22.

43. BC (Letter 242, To Horkheimer, September 16, 1934), 456–457.

44. GS, volume 7, part 2, 860, as quoted in AB, 28.

45. BC (Letter 14, March 9, 1934), 28–29.

46. CB (Letter to Adorno, May 31, 1935), 488–491, quote from 488.

47. AP (Q Panorama), 533. I have revised the translation based on GS, volume 5, part 2, 661; emphasis added.

48. AB (Letter 35, Benjamin to Adorno, June 10, 1935), 98–101, quote from 101.

49. BC (Letter 266, To Horkheimer, October 16, 1935), 508–510, quote from 509.

50. WM, 45.

51. BC (Letter 263, Adorno to Benjamin, August 2, 1935), 494–503, quotes from 495, 503.

52. The shift is also noted by Eiland and Jennings; see EJ, 494–495.

53. WM, "The Paris of the Second Empire in Baudelaire," 46–133, quote from 47.

54. WM, 66. The original translation of this Benjamin text is by Harry Zohn. But I have not reproduced the English translation of the passage from Baudelaire's poem that is found in the Zohn version. Instead, I have translated the French passage from Baudelaire's poem myself, relying on the expertise of my friend and colleague Arthur Goldhammer, whose assistance I'm pleased to acknowledge here.

55. WM, 85.

56. WM, 108.

57. WM, 108–109.

58. WM, 127.

59. AB (Letter 110, November 10, 1938), 283.

60. WM, "Introduction" by Michael Jennings, 19.

61. AB (Letter 110, November 10, 1938), 286.

62. BC (Letter 247, To Alfred Cohn, December 19, 1934), 464–466.

63. BC (Letter 256, To Max Horkheimer), 480–481.

64. Vicki Caron, "The Antisemitic Revival in France in the 1930s," *Journal of Modern History* 70, no. 1 (March 1998): 24–73; see esp. 30.

65. Caron, "The Antisemitic Revival in France in the 1930s," 39–40.

66. For details see the online historical resource of the United States Holocaust Memorial Museum (https://encyclopedia.ushmm.org/content/en/article/the-united-states-and-the-refugee-crisis-1938-41, consulted August 7, 2024).

67. SB (Letter 83, Scholem to Benjamin, June 6, 1936), 180–181.

68. For more on Scholem's role in Brit Shalom, see David Biale, *Gershom Scholem: Master of the Kabbalah* (New Haven: Yale University Press, 2018), esp. 95–97.

69. SB (Letter 85, Scholem to Benjamin, August 26, 1936), 183–185, quote 184.

70. SB (Letter 84, Benjamin to Scholem, June 25, 1936), 182–183.

71. Caron, "The Antisemitic Revival in France in the 1930s," 53.

72. See the sequence of letters in SB (Letters 92–95, May 7, 1937–August 5, 1937), 195–203. On Benjamin's passport, see SB (Letter 97, Benjamin to Scholem, September 6, 1937), 205.

73. SB (Letter 99, Benjamin to Scholem, November 20, 1937), 208.

74. AB (Letter to Th. and Gretel Adorno, June 19, 1938), 260.

75. "Curriculum Vitae V," GS, volume 4, editorial notes, 775–777.

76. "Eduard Fuchs, Collector and Historian," SW, 3:260–302, quote from 276.

77. "Eduard Fuchs, Collector and Historian," SW, 3:260–302, quote from 284.

78. "Eduard Fuchs, Collector and Historian," SW, 3:260–302, quote from 267.

79. WM, "Central Park," 134–169, quote from 145.

80. WM, "Central Park," 161. My translation based on GS, volume 1, part 2, 655–690, quote from 683.

81. GB (Letter 1307, August 1, 1940), 6:312–314.

82. WM, "On Some Motifs in Baudelaire," 198.

83. For a historical study of the term and especially on the debates between Adorno and Benjamin, see Martin Jay, *Songs of Experience: Modern American and European Variations on a Universal Theme* (Berkeley: University of California Press, 2005), esp. ch. 8, "Lamenting the Crisis of Experience: Benjamin and Adorno," 312–360.

84. WM, "On Some Motifs in Baudelaire," 171–172, 178.

85. WM, "On Some Motifs in Baudelaire," 209–210, translation modified.

86. CB (Letter 318, To Adorno, August 6, 1939), 611–613, quote from 612.

87. GB (Letter to Horkheimer, May 16, 1939), 6:279–283, esp. 282.

88. GB (Letter to Lackner, June 4, 1939), 6:286–290. On Lackner's career, see Christian Lenz, editor, *Stephan Lackner—der Freund Max Beckmanns*, Katalog zur Ausstellung des Max Beckmann Archivs in der Staatsgalerie moderner Kunst München, February 3–April 9, 2000.

89. SF, 213.

90. MB, 240.

Epilogue

1. GB (Letter 1316, To Horkheimer, September 4, 1939), 6:332–333.

2. Max Horkheimer, "Die Juden und Europa," *Studies in Philosophy and Social Science* 8 (1939): 115–137.

3. Quoted from Horkheimer, "The Jews and Europe," in *The Frankfurt School on Religion: Key Writings by the Major Thinkers*, edited by Eduardo Mendieta (New York: Routledge, 2005), 225–241, quote from 241. SB (Letter 128, Scholem to Benjamin, February

1940), 264–265. Despite its rather crude explanatory framework, however, the essay ends with lines that merit reading: "The Jews were once proud of abstract monotheism, their rejection of idolatry, their refusal to make something finite an absolute. Their distress today points them back. Disrespect for anything mortal that puffs itself up as a god is the religion of those who cannot resist devoting their life to the preparation of something better, even in the Europe of the Iron Heel." For the letter that prompted Scholem's response, see SB (Letter 127, January 11, 1940), 262–264; esp. 263. For the general context, see Jack Jacobs, "1939: Max Horkheimer's 'Die Juden und Europa' Appears," in *Yale Companion to Jewish Writing and Thought in German Culture, 1096–1996*, ed. Sander L. Gilman and Jack Zipes (New Haven: Yale University Press, 1997), 571–576. For a critique, see Martin Jay, "The Jews and the Frankfurt School: Critical Theory's Analysis of Anti-Semitism," in *Permanent Exiles: Essays on the Intellectual Migration from Germany to America* (New York: Columbia University Press, 1986), 90–100.

4. SB (Letter 128, Scholem to Benjamin, February 1940), 264–265. For the letter that prompted Scholem's response, see SB (Letter 127, January 11, 1940), 262–264; esp. 263.

5. For information on Adrienne Monnier, see the editorial note in GB, 4:103–104.

6. GB (Letter to Adrienne Monnier, September 21, 1939), 6:333–335; see note at 335.

7. GB (Letter to Gretel Adorno, October 12, 1939), 6:343.

8. GB (Letter to Sylvia Beach, October 20, 1939), 6:346–347.

9. Hans Sahl, "Walter Benjamin in the Internment Camp," in OB, 346–352.

10. Hans Sahl, "Walter Benjamin in the Internment Camp," in OB, 346–352, 349–350.

11. GB (Letter to Scholem, November 25, 1939), 6:358–359.

12. GB (Letter to Stephan Lackner, December 13, 1939), 6:365–367.

13. See the editorial notes in GB, 6:371–372.

14. GB (Letter to Cecilia Razovsky, December 14, 1939), 6:372.

15. GB (Letter to Gretel Adorno, December 14, 1939), 6:367–368.

16. Jeffrey A. Grossman, "France as Wahlheimat for Two German Jews: Heinrich Heine and Walter Benjamin," in *Spiritual Homelands: The Cultural Experience of Exile, Place and Displacement Among Jews and Others*, edited by Asher D. Biemann, Richard I. Cohen, and Sarah E. Wobick-Segev (Berlin: Walter De Gruyter, 2020), 153–182.

17. GB (Letter to Horkheimer, December 15, 1939), 6:373–376.

18. GB, 6:375–376, as quoted from Max Horkheimer, *Briefwechsel, 1937–1940*, edited by Gunzelin Schmid Noerr (Frankfurt am Main: Fischer Verlag, 1995), 690.

19. See, e.g., GB (Letter 1342, To Gretel Adorno, January 17, 1940), 6:382–388.

20. GB (Letter 1350, To Horkheimer, February 22, 1940), 6:399–402, quote from 400.

21. "On the Concept of History," SW, 4:389–400; also see the "Paralipomena," 401–411.

22. On chess playing and the philosophy of history, see Seyla Benhabib, *Exile, Statelessness, and Migration: Playing Chess with History from Hannah Arendt to Isaiah Berlin* (Princeton: Princeton University Press, 2018), esp. ch. 3, p. 34 and ff.

23. "Paralipomena," SW, 4:401–411; esp. 401.

24. "On the Concept of History," SW, 4:390.

25. "On the Concept of History," SW, 4:392.

26. "On the Concept of History," SW, 4:392.

27. "On the Concept of History," SW, 4:395.

28. "On the Concept of History," SW, 4:395; for comments on the provenance of this text see 400n28.

29. GB (Letter to Horkheimer, March 23, 1940), 6:403–423.

30. CB (Letter to Adorno, May 7, 1940), 628–635.

31. GB, 6:397; CB (Letter 328, To Adorno, May 7, 1940), 628–635; BC (Letter 327, To Gretel Adorno, January 17, 1940), 625–628; GB (Letter 1360, To Lackner, May 5, 2024), 6:441–444, quote from 442.

32. Marc Bloch, *L'Étrange Défaite: Témoinage écrit en 1940* (Société des Éditions Franc-Tireur, 1946).

33. EJ, 667–668; MB, 251.

34. GB, 6:466.

35. BC (Letter 331, To Hannah Arendt, July 8, 1940), 637.

36. BC (Letter 332, To Adorno, August 2, 1940), 637–638.

37. GB (Letter 1375, To Hilde Schröder, August 22, 1940), 4:480–481.

38. LF, 106. Scholars have continued to puzzle over the question of what was in the briefcase. The most likely answer is that it contained his drafts for the "Theses" on history. For an account of the mystery, see Giorgio van Straten, "Lost in Migration," https://aeon.co/essays/what-happened-to-walter-benjamins-precious-black-suitcase.

Afterword

1. Hannah Arendt, "Introduction. Walter Benjamin: 1892–1940," in *Illuminations*, Hannah Arendt, ed., Harry Zohn, trans. (New York: Schocken, 1969), 18.

2. This is the topic of a wonderfully exploratory and insightful essay by Benjamin Aldes Wurgaft, to whom I am very much indebted: Benjamin Aldes Wurgaft, "The Uses of Walter: Walter Benjamin and the Counterfactual Imagination," *History and Theory* 49, no. 3 (2010): 361–383.

3. T. J. Clark, "Should Benjamin Have Read Marx?" *boundary 2* 30:1 (2003): 31–49.

4. It is true, however, that the various members of the Frankfurt School felt some sense of solidarity or sympathy with Israel. For this theme, see Jack Jacobs, *The Frankfurt School, Jewish Lives, and Anti-Semitism* (Cambridge: Cambridge University Press, 2015). Also see Theodor W. Adorno, *Fighting Antisemitism Today: A Lecture*, translated by Wieland Hoban (Polity Books, 2025); and for relevance to debates over anti-Semitism and Zionism today, see my afterword in this edition, 44–68.

ACKNOWLEDGMENTS

IN THE CONCEPTION and composition of this book I acquired many debts. An initial source of inspiration came from my encounter with a book by Daniel Mendelsohn, *Three Rings: A Tale of Exile, Narrative, and Fate* (New York: New York Review Books, 2020). Mendelsohn's study introduced me to the idea of "ring composition," a narrative device that scholars have found in Homer's writing. For reasons of accessibility I have made only minimal use of this device here, but it has nonetheless inspired me a great deal, and it has assisted me in breaking free of the linear constraints that biographers typically obey. No less significant was *The Dialectics of Seeing: Walter Benjamin and the Arcades Project*, by Susan Buck-Morss, a study that is widely esteemed both for its unique manner of composition and its incomparable insights into Benjamin's unfinished masterpiece. I owe perhaps my greatest debt, however, to three superb biographies that were published well before this one. They include *Walter Benjamin: A Critical Life*, by Howard Eiland and Michael Jennings; *Walter Benjamin: A Biography*, by Momme Brodersen; and *Walter Benjamin: An Intellectual Biography*, by Bernd Witte. All three of these books have served as guides for me as I explored the details of an exceedingly complex life.

For the monumental task of creating a workable chronology, I owe enormous thanks to Rosaline DeLaura, who was at that time a student in Harvard College. I would also like to thank Michael Mango, a doctoral student in religious studies at Harvard, with whom I have had the great pleasure of co-teaching a seminar on Benjamin, and whose brilliant dissertation has revealed Benjamin's work in a new and unfamiliar light. I would also like to express my gratitude to the students in the seminar, which convened in Harvard College in the fall of 2022. The autumn of that particular year was one of great personal tragedy for me, but I found that working with students was a source of much comfort that assisted me in regaining some of my much-needed equilibrium.

For assistance in research and guidance to unknown sources, I am grateful to Rob Kaufman, Derek Penslar, and the great many scholars who have written so insightfully on Walter Benjamin over the past decades. I cannot mention all of those scholars here, but I trust they will detect the many places where I have drawn instruction from their work. I owe a very special thanks to the directors and assistants at the Walter Benjamin Archiv in Berlin, especially Michael Schwarz, Julia Bernhard, and Oliver Kunisch.

I owe a very special thanks to Ileene Smith, the editorial director of the Jewish Lives series, who first suggested that I might be interested in writing for the series. I am also grateful to the series editors, Anita Shapira and Steven J. Zipperstein. To all of the editors and managers associated with the series I must express my deepest gratitude for their patience and sympathies for a project that took me far too many years, while other commitments both personal and professional consumed my time. Warmest thanks to the editors at Yale University Press, including Heather Gold, Jennifer Banks, and Phillip King. I am also grateful to my agent, Molly Atlas, for her assistance and advice over these many years.

For his encouragement and careful reading of the final manuscript I am grateful as always to Martin Jay, my mentor and friend.

Finally, I would like to express my deepest gratitude to Shterna Friedman, my companion, my interlocutor, and my miracle, who appeared in my life at a time when miracles seemed impossible. You are my own star of redemption, and this book is dedicated to you.

INDEX

Page numbers in italics refer to illustrations

Jewish Lives is a prizewinning series of interpretive biography designed to explore the many facets of Jewish identity. Individual volumes illuminate the imprint of Jewish figures upon literature, religion, philosophy, politics, cultural and economic life, and the arts and sciences. Subjects are paired with authors to elicit lively, deeply informed books that explore the range and depth of the Jewish experience
from antiquity to the present.

Jewish Lives is a partnership of Yale University Press and the Leon D. Black Foundation. Ileene Smith is editorial director. Anita Shapira and Steven J. Zipperstein are series editors.

PUBLISHED TITLES INCLUDE:

Abraham: The First Jew, by Anthony Julius
Rabbi Akiva: Sage of the Talmud, by Barry W. Holtz
Ben-Gurion: Father of Modern Israel, by Anita Shapira
Judah Benjamin: Counselor to the Confederacy, by James Traub
Bernard Berenson: A Life in the Picture Trade, by Rachel Cohen
Irving Berlin: New York Genius, by James Kaplan
Sarah: The Life of Sarah Bernhardt, by Robert Gottlieb
Leonard Bernstein: An American Musician, by Allen Shawn
Hayim Nahman Bialik: Poet of Hebrew, by Avner Holtzman
Léon Blum: Prime Minister, Socialist, Zionist, by Pierre Birnbaum
Franz Boas: In Praise of Open Minds, by Noga Arikha
Louis D. Brandeis: American Prophet, by Jeffrey Rosen
Mel Brooks: Disobedient Jew, by Jeremy Dauber
Martin Buber: A Life of Faith and Dissent, by Paul Mendes-Flohr
David: The Divided Heart, by David Wolpe
Moshe Dayan: Israel's Controversial Hero, by Mordechai Bar-On
Disraeli: The Novel Politician, by David Cesarani
Alfred Dreyfus: The Man at the Center of the Affair, by Maurice Samuels
Einstein: His Space and Times, by Steven Gimbel
Becoming Elijah: Prophet of Transformation, by Daniel Matt
The Many Lives of Anne Frank, by Ruth Franklin
Becoming Freud: The Making of a Psychoanalyst, by Adam Phillips
Betty Friedan: Magnificent Disrupter, by Rachel Shteir

Emma Goldman: Revolution as a Way of Life, by Vivian Gornick
Hank Greenberg: The Hero Who Didn't Want to Be One, by Mark Kurlansky
Peggy Guggenheim: The Shock of the Modern, by Francine Prose
Ben Hecht: Fighting Words, Moving Pictures, by Adina Hoffman
Heinrich Heine: Writing the Revolution, by George Prochnik
Lillian Hellman: An Imperious Life, by Dorothy Gallagher
Herod the Great: Jewish King in a Roman World, by Martin Goodman
Theodor Herzl: The Charismatic Leader, by Derek Penslar
Abraham Joshua Heschel: A Life of Radical Amazement, by Julian Zelizer
Houdini: The Elusive American, by Adam Begley
Jabotinsky: A Life, by Hillel Halkin
Jacob: Unexpected Patriarch, by Yair Zakovitch
Franz Kafka: The Poet of Shame and Guilt, by Saul Friedländer
Carole King: She Made the Earth Move, by Jane Eisner
Rav Kook: Mystic in a Time of Revolution, by Yehudah Mirsky
Stanley Kubrick: American Filmmaker, by David Mikics
Stan Lee: A Life in Comics, by Liel Leibovitz
Primo Levi: The Matter of a Life, by Berel Lang
Maimonides: Faith in Reason, by Alberto Manguel
Groucho Marx: The Comedy of Existence, by Lee Siegel
Karl Marx: Philosophy and Revolution, by Shlomo Avineri
Louis B. Mayer and Irving Thalberg: The Whole Equation, by Kenneth Turan
Golda Meir: Israel's Matriarch, by Deborah E. Lipstadt
Menasseh ben Israel: Rabbi of Amsterdam, by Steven Nadler
Moses Mendelssohn: Sage of Modernity, by Shmuel Feiner
Harvey Milk: His Lives and Death, by Lillian Faderman
Arthur Miller: American Witness, by John Lahr

Moses: A Human Life, by Avivah Gottlieb Zornberg
Amos Oz: Writer, Activist, Icon, by Robert Alter
Proust: The Search, by Benjamin Taylor
Yitzhak Rabin: Soldier, Leader, Statesman, by Itamar Rabinovich
Ayn Rand: Writing a Gospel of Success, by Alexandra Popoff
Walther Rathenau: Weimar's Fallen Statesman,
by Shulamit Volkov
Man Ray: The Artist and His Shadows, by Arthur Lubow
Sidney Reilly: Master Spy, by Benny Morris
Admiral Hyman Rickover: Engineer of Power, by Marc Wortman
Jerome Robbins: A Life in Dance, by Wendy Lesser
Julius Rosenwald: Repairing the World, by Hasia R. Diner
Philip Roth: Stung by Life, by Steven J. Zipperstein
Mark Rothko: Toward the Light in the Chapel,
by Annie Cohen-Solal
Ruth: A Migrant's Tale, by Ilana Pardes
Menachem Mendel Schneerson: Becoming the Messiah,
by Ezra Glinter
Gershom Scholem: Master of the Kabbalah, by David Biale
Bugsy Siegel: The Dark Side of the American Dream,
by Michael Shnayerson
Solomon: The Lure of Wisdom, by Steven Weitzman
Stephen Sondheim: Art Isn't Easy, by Daniel Okrent
Steven Spielberg: A Life in Films, by Molly Haskell
Spinoza: Freedom's Messiah, by Ian Buruma
Alfred Stieglitz: Taking Pictures, Making Painters, by Phyllis Rose
Barbra Streisand: Redefining Beauty, Femininity, and Power,
by Neal Gabler
Henrietta Szold: Hadassah and the Zionist Dream,
by Francine Klagsbrun
Leon Trotsky: A Revolutionary's Life, by Joshua Rubenstein